AMERICA...
SPELLS
...I AM RACE

Born to a Life of Strife

By
Gerard A. Matthews

Copyright © 2025 by Gerard A. Matthews

All rights reserved.

ISBN: 979-8-89324-766-4

No part of this book may be reproduced, stored in a retrieval system, or transmitted in any form or by any means—electronic, mechanical, photocopying, recording, or otherwise—without prior written permission of the publisher, except for brief quotations used in reviews or articles.

The opinions expressed by the Author are not necessarily those held by the Publishers.

The information contained within this book is strictly for informational purposes. The material may include information, products, or services by third parties. As such, the Author and Publisher do not assume responsibility or liability for any third-party material or opinions. The publisher is not responsible for websites (or their content) that are not owned by the publisher. Readers are advised to do their own due diligence when it comes to making decisions.

Published by Franklin Publishers

Printed in the United States of America

For permissions, inquiries, or additional copies, contact:

Franklin Publishers

www.franklinpublishers.com

The word "AMERICA" reconfigured spells... "I AM RACE." This indicting assessment of the lack of racial progress in the USA from its inception to this very instant documents and chronicles events that demonstrate where and how America actually failed to achieve its greatness potential, let alone be made great again. The book highlights a variety of documented and suspiciously well-hidden reiterations of racial injustices and setbacks affecting these people that support the country's lack of greatness while outlining the anguished feelings caused by the fluid changes of racism constantly re-emerging and re-inventing itself every few years, causing the ongoing sufferings and struggles to the American people of "Alkebulan" aka African heritage via slavery.

This untold perspective addresses and only scratches the surface of the many ongoing issues affecting this one of perhaps tens of millions of peoples' journey chronicled from the African continent through the founding of this country, its enslavement period, the twists and turns of the lack of a proper Reconstruction, the results of Jim Crow to "Separate but Equal," through the Civil Rights movement and legislation, up to the death of George Floyd. He reveals a "Racial System of White Supremacy" that's rooted in the country, resulting in these peoples' unrelentingly ill, unequaled, and unparalleled mistreatment while challenging and encouraging all people everywhere and, particularly Americans, whose descendants are of the colonizing founding fathers, to take an honest look at ourselves and their role in it all from 1619-...?

AMERICA anagrammed is: I AM RACE

...Then he pulled his earbuds out, turned, and balled his fist tight as his chest heaved up. He looked down at me, dead into my eyes, with eyes full of anger and rage, and within inches of my face and shouted, "Fuck you Nigger, I don't give a fuck!" He didn't say "nigga," "niggra," or "nigglet," the other derivation I've heard. I had seen this crazy, hateful look before and remembered the overwhelming fear I felt before fleeing.

It was then I experienced the psychological reaction known as "Fight or Flight" and also that out-of-body experience when you're there, but it's as if you're also watching it unfold from a different vantage point. It can only be compared to when people speak of a near-death experience, where they briefly died, then revived and able to describe what went on in the room while they were "dead." Suddenly felt all alone and saw nothing but white light. Then, an intense rush of heat consumed my body as my fist balled up. I had been here before, in this position of fight or flight, but this time, I wasn't about to run...

Table of Contents

Dedications and Acknowledgements		vi
About the Author		viii
Forewords		ix
Introduction		xi
Preface		xiii
Prelude:	Before the story unfolds	xvi
Chapter: 0:	A starting point	1
Chapter: 1:	When you point the finger at someone, you've got three fingers pointing back at you…	33
Chapter: 2:	A m e r i c a……I am R a c e	73
Chapter: 3:	Fundamental foundational formations	103
Chapter: 4:	Segregation good…Integration bad	110
Chapter: 5:	Feel as if anything is possible, then…	124
Chapter: 6:	Racist people have a mental problem and hate themselves……But they can be healed!	144
Chapter: 7:	The angry Black Man: myth or manufactured?	158
Chapter: 8:	Donald Skunk…	160
Prologue:	Malcolm or Martin	174
Afterwords		176
Bibliography		180

DEDICATIONS AND ACKNOWLEDGEMENTS

Being the GOD-fearing man I am, I first acknowledge my "Creator and Almighty GOD." I recognize and Thank "GOD," the author of LOVE, for giving me life, breath, and the strength to do anything, who inspires the individual creativity in each of us. And as the "Creator," has demonstrated throughout the vast creativity of the Universes both seen and unknown. Without the Spirit of God in me, which is a "Holy Spirit," I wouldn't be able to do a single thing. It is by the "Grace of God" I am alive today after suffering a stroke in July of 2018 affecting the left side of my body. I recognize I could easily be pushing up daises.

And although I haven't been able to resume all my former routines in the same manner, it is "GOD" who has granted me these additional years and the idea to write this book and so much more. He has restored and brought a "Prodigal Son " back home to welcoming arms, and I'm eternally grateful. By whatever name you call God or whether you believe in God or not, it's important to remember that each day above dirt, is the most valuable precious of gifts that shouldn't be squandered. With that, as in my past, I honestly try to live by the "Golden Rule," trying my best to treat everyone fairly and hoping everybody's trying to do the same.

Equally important, this book is dedicated first and foremost TO MY MOTHER, the strongest person I ever bore witness to. For your unquestionable LOVE, dedication, sacrifices, and support of your children and most important priority. Thank you for your insistent emphasis on education, your unrelenting drive, and work ethic. Finally, I THANK YOU for the unnecessary sufferings and struggles you endured during your lifetime. I LOVE YOU ALWAYS, MOTHER, not to death but through death!

Also, "Special Thanks" and dedication to the four most influential Teachers in my life in the order they entered, for their motivational impact and the influence they've had on shaping my personal and educational Outlook and Life Experiences. To my 7th grade classroom teacher with a background in Art, Ms. Katherine (Kathy) Legrand who forever altered my educational goals to do my very best at every educational opportunity; to the most influential and continuing relationship, my High School Band Director, father figure and friend Mr. William Johnson, who also shares my heritage, respectively along with two professors from Livingstone College, Dr. Charlotte Fitzgerald a Psychology Professor who personally took time to educate me on Black women in Jazz and Author Dr. Mattie Lakin, who provided me with one on one instruction.

A "Very Special Thank You" goes to my longtime friend, Minister, and additional father figure, Mr. Eugene Dumas. You have demonstrated God's Holy Spirit with actions that made me realize: A friend in need is truly a friend in deed.

Last but not least, I dedicate this book To All My "Ancestors" who were bought and brought, sacrificed and suffered, born and buried from our Mother continent of Alkebulan, down through our entire linage of those enslaved and afterward segregated, Jim Crowed and lynched, some for entertainment at "picnics" on Sundays and to those existing and enduring today, who marched for "Civil Rights," as well as contemporaries, marching for all lives mattering with "Black Lives Matter," in this country called the United States of America, from our forced landing on these shores in 1619 until...When?

Of note, I heard a saying somewhere and read some material stating the origin of the word "picnic" comes from a shortened version of the phrase "pick a nigger." You'll hear what I'm talking about if you say it over and over a few times really fast. It was customary to pick a black man to Lynch for the entertainment portion of these regular after church gatherings.

ABOUT THE AUTHOR

Gerard A. Matthews is native to Chicago, and Music Major graduate of Simeon (Vocational) High School, and an alumni of the Chicago All-City Band. After earning a full scholarship to Livingstone College and before receiving his Bachelor's Degree in Music Performance, Gerard, a member of Phi Beta Sigma Fraternity Inc., also served 4 years in the Salisbury/Rowan Symphony Orchestra on Flute & Piccolo, a 2-time guest conductor, and a featured guest soloist. In 1983, he recorded with the internationally recognized group "Smoke City" on CBS Records/Epic label, charting in Billboard's "Top 100," then went on to perform in and around Chicago, around the country, and overseas.

Gerard earned his Illinois Teacher Certification K-12 in 1993, then served the Chicago Public Schools for over 24 years both as a General/Instrumental Music Instructor and as the initial Principal Conductor for the Chicago All-City Elementary Concert Band for 14 years. He's directed the Soundmine Merchants Jazz/R&B big band since 2008, a group that has been performing since the 1960s. Gerard also performs with a number of other top-notched groups in and around Chicago, including "Noteworthy," the Chicago Public School Teacher's Jazz Band, and Michael Ross and the Boss 8.

Understanding that we are all brethren and that God has blessed me through Livingstone College by awarding scholarships to people of and outside my heritage, thereby allowing me to graduate with zero college debt, and because of people like Mr. Dumas helping me during the most difficult period of my life and finally because of the millions of people who have been born into impoverished conditions beyond their control, with others of and outside my heritage falling into circumstances like incarcerations or addictions that require them needing a second chance, God has given me a blueprint for returning the blessings whenever and however I can.

FOREWORDS

I understand and readily accept the inevitable fact that this book won't be popular with many people(s) of the various populations/heritages in America, including some from my own. I anticipate the book will be viewed as biased, controversial, hateful, or skewed by some. If so, **IT IS NOT INTENTIONAL.** I honor all viewpoints as I ask you to honor mine, understanding we don't all share a common upbringing. I'm simply regurgitating what I've ingested. It is MY HOPE that this book might be helpful to ALL PEOPLE, especially to those NOT sharing my heritage. The book is meant to shed additional light on and raise awareness to the unrelentingly tough and difficult struggles of a shared plight of people as I see and understand it.

It is NOT INTENDED to provoke anger, raise anyone's ire, or be hateful or spiteful. Nevertheless, I'm certain SOME INDIVIDUALS will ignore the previous statement and purposefully take parts of these writings out of context and quote me in an attempt to stir up like-minded people for the purposes of inciting further violence and cite me as the perpetrator. These will be the same type of people who "choose" ignorance and hatred to justify their desire to circumvent the rule of law and to assume the power they feel is being stolen from them as a part of their "god-given" rights in this country.

It is MY HOPE this book will raise the level of empathy and sympathy, as well as sensitivity and understanding to all the people of this country and, by extension, to the world that will forge a change from a hardened heart into a "Heart of Love," in those who may disagree, in the hope that something like this will never happen again anywhere to any people, and not to just recognize, but to realize and put into practice, the extension of Equality to all of Humanity.

Finally, as a result of my personal experiences, I dare say that Humanity would continue to treat each other with this level of disdain and hatred if we were confronted with an attack from an entity outside the realm of humanity whose Origins are from other places in the known and unknown Universe. I dare say that a true "Brotherhood of Humanity" would be forged. But honestly, it shouldn't have come to that!

INTRODUCTION

Who and what qualifies me to speak on this? You qualify me because I'm just like you, the "average Joe," your public school classmate and neighborhood friend claiming no special status or privilege. With that said, this book is MY PERSONAL INTERPRETATION of the many racial issues I've observed, often personally confronted, and historically learned about during my life's experience. Based on the common sense of reasoning, logic, observation, and deduction bestowed Me by our Almighty Creator God, combined with my individual development and then applied to the different sets of circumstances I've confronted.

In previous years, I made that statement on my "FaKebook" page, "What's on your mind," where I also proclaimed, "common sense ain't common these days," and that I don't represent any club, group, organization, or political affiliation. I will further say that I only speak for myself and not for all the people who share my Heritage. However, I wouldn't be surprised if others of my heritage share some of these thoughts and feelings as well because we historically share many common experiences. For example, me simply writing three letters, "DWB," meaning "Driving While Black," evokes a common happenstance.

I want to clearly state that, although this book will emphasize many racial issues and injustices that the peoples of my heritage have had to contend with since our trade-off and abduction into this country, I'm NOT SAYING that "ALL" the DESCENDENTS of the colonizing European countries" (the so-called, "white people") in America today, are guilty of practicing the racial injustices that are obviously still present and prevalent. I'm NOT

STEREOTYPING any group, race, or ethnicity, and I never consider anything written here to be inclusive or representative of an entire race or ethnicity!

There is no stereotyping intended here and no "all" of anything, anyone, or any group, as there are always the "exceptions to the rules." Obviously, I'm unable to put a scientifically accurate number on this, and I acknowledge and recognize that in my everyday life, there are significant and substantial numbers, and I would go so far as to say the majority of "white people" who believe in and practice equality in their everyday lives, and unquestionably espouse the "promised principles" that America is based on, as stated in our Constitution. I call it "common sense" reigning again.

Lastly, I will only be able to scratch the surface of any topic or issue I've selected confronting me and what "we" collectively face and endure. Otherwise, the book would become as thick as a hard cover Webster's Dictionary and seemingly unending because the racial issues in the country have not ended and, in many ways recently, have escalated. Finally, because so much of our collective history has been purposefully buried, both the known and unexcavated information would, in and of itself, fill volumes.

PREFACE

During the course of history, several other ethnicities have labeled the people of my heritage with a wide variety of names to identify us as an ethnic group that includes Africans, African-Americans, Afro-Americans, Blacks, Black and Brown people, Colored, Negro, and People of Color. Within my own community, I've heard us referred to as "Moors," like what Martin Lawrence was called in the movie "Black Knight." With such a large list of labels, some talk of our identity crises. So, I won't use any of them and opt to use phrases like "The people who share my heritage" or "the forcibly imported people (of my heritage)," etc.... It's my attempt to not allow any other people to identify ME or the collective "we." Indulge me to add just one more name to this mixed-matched list! Alkebulan or Akebulan, for which I will explain in further detail shortly.

I use the word "slaveholder" over slave owner because humans don't own other humans. They may have traded whatever valuables, but they never owned them. They were only "holding" them. They held them against their will. If they hadn't forcibly held them, those enslaved would have never remained in their custody, as there were many known and unknown rebellions and attempts to escape. I prefer to use "enslaved" over slave because the enslavement was "enforced."

I will refer to the "American Indians" as our "Native or Indigenous" peoples or populations (although historical documentation reveals they also migrated via the Bering Strait and by the natural current patterns of the Atlantic Ocean from the "Mother" continent). I might use some phrases like, "I heard it said somewhere," or "what I heard was." Perhaps, "What I was told was," etc... to indicate it's not something I said but something I heard from elsewhere. When

I use the word "America," I'm referring to the United States and not to north, central, or South America.

I have tendencies toward wordplay, and I sometimes "nickname" people, places, and things. It's a habit I unknowingly picked up during my first teaching experience in a Spanish-speaking community to help me recognize and pronounce some names. I would create a beat on my desk, then "Rap" the students' names or nicknames. I realized they loved it because if I didn't, they insisted I start at the beginning and do what I always did.

Because I often see people being phony on the social media platform "Facebook," I call it "FaKebook." Donald Trump is nicknamed Donald Skunk or $kunk. George W. Bush was already George "Dummy" Bush, and his father was "Daddy Bush." "Ditch Bitch" Mitch McConnell may be called out, and there may be others. Sometimes, I have my reasons for nicknaming, but often, it's just my corny attempt at humor. Another idiosyncrasy of mine is the use of wordplay, as demonstrated in Chapter 7. Finally, I ask that you bear with me, as I will use lots of "quotation marks." Due to the sensitive nature of the book, I'm trying to be as specific as possible.

The book is not intended to be a deep intellectual study into the psyche of man. It's basically my off-the-cuff personal observation of his actions and reactions to an ever-changing world, primarily as it relates to the people who share my heritage in this country. It's meant to tease you with tidbits of information and I invite you to explore the subject matter more deeply at your own convenience. However, as historical validity necessitates, there are instances where truthful, clear, and concise concrete conclusions must be levied and, therefore, documented for the record because sometimes there is the need to verify information with actual documentation. Just the facts, Jack!

Because we've been afforded the luxury of the "internet," I thought I'd take advantage it. Sometimes, I'll indicate the information was gathered via a Google search. A brief story behind why I will sometimes use Google. During my time in High School, a requirement for graduation was to complete a "research" paper for your English Class. It was normally written during your senior year. You were given about 2 months to complete the paper then defend it with your oral arguments. It required spending multiple hours at the public library going through microfilm, reading periodicals, then finding and reading books to take out for additional home study and research.

That year, I also chose as an elective a "Black Civics" class, which, unbeknownst to me, also required the research paper. So, I had two of them to research, write and defend at the same time. After several days agonizing over what subjects to write about, I had a flash of brilliance and decided to combine the English and Black Civics classes and write my papers on what was then called "Black English, the way Black people talk," which was also called "slang," and today is known as "Ebonics." I found it to be an interesting topic that gave me some insightful "purported" explanation and understanding as to why the people of my heritage generally speak the way we do.

Needless to say, I didn't share that information with my either of my teachers and I'm pleased to report the paper was academically sound and consistent, receiving grades of 95% and 97% respectively. I mention this because, although much of the factual information listed in this book is information I have read in the traditional manner, I Thank God for Google. There will be limited use of profanity and of the word "Nigger," which I feel is necessary for its historical context. This is done to emphasize or make a point and not to be vulgar. Some redundancy will occur to emphasize certain points I want to drive home and not forgotten along the way. Also at times, I will introduce an idea and meander a bit, before returning to it several paragraphs later.

The book is subtitled "Born to a Life of Strife." However, it was the second working title. The original title was "Life of Strife" with "AMERICA…I AM RACE" being Chapter 2. But after writing most of the book, I shared the concept with one of my oldest friends. He suggested I turn Chapter 2 into the title because it was more "catchy" to him. I thought it over and agreed. Thank you Michael G for that. I now invite you through your empathy, to experience just a little of my (our) strife and sufferings resulting from these seemingly never ending constantly inflicted twists and turns that have become our unrelenting trials and tribulations.

Prelude

BEFORE THE STORY UNFOLDS
(Systemic and Systematic)

When I first thought to write this book in January of 2016, it was partly due to the election of former president Skunk and partly due to the incident I wrote about at the beginning of the book underneath the title because they occurred almost simultaneously. But like most of us, I quickly got caught up in the fast and furious shenanigans of the former president, so, ironically, it became the main reason I didn't start it until October 2021.

Terms like "Systemic Racism" and "Critical Race Theory," aka (CRT) weren't yet common to our cultural vernacular. At that time, I had a DVD that was either the predecessor to or contemporary of Systemic Racism. I also felt what was being packaged as "CRT" was what should've been part of basic US History. Otherwise, it was being "whitewashed" or watered down. My understanding of systemic racism, which hadn't been as clearly defined at the time, was forged later through some fortunate contacts and developed relationships with older and wiser individuals who compelled me to seek additional information for myself.

With regard to "Systemic Racism," the DVD I owned was entitled "Racial System of White Supremacy," of which I will abbreviate as (RSWS). I consider this information as the defining classifier of "Systemic Racism" as it also relates to "Critical Race Theory." The 9 defining identifying categories alphabetically are:

1. Economic
2. Education
3. Entertainment
4. Labor
5. Law
6. Political
7. Religion
8. Sex
9. War

As I continue writing, I will identify these categories as they apply by using, for example, (RSWS: 4) or (RSWS: 1, 3, & 6) if more than one is applicable at the time.

I decided to Google the definition of "Systemic." The first listing stated relating to a system, especially as opposed to a particular part; relating or common to a system, such as affecting the body with disease. For example, the "Circulatory" and "Respiratory" are full systems within our bodies. The lungs are part of the respiratory system, whereas veins are part of the circulatory system. Some synonyms for systemic include structural, comprehensive, inherent, pervasive, and extensively ingrained.

What is systemic in government? That's something affecting the whole of government rather than just a part or when corruption extends throughout the entire government rather than to just one, two, or a few individuals. Systemic discrimination is defined as the practices or attitudes that have, whether by design or impact, the effect of limiting an individual's or group's right to the opportunities generally available because of attributed rather than actual characteristics.

The difference between systemic and systematic is that systematic is the older, more common word, describing something that is done according to a set method or in an orderly way. Systemic is more comprehensive and relates to affecting an entire system. While both can be used broadly, when relating to a system, their actual practices are distinct. While there's nothing inherently wrong with either word, systemic, when used as an adjective, it's usually used in a negative connotation.

What makes an issue systemic is the consequence of problems inherent in the overall system rather than a specific or isolated incident. In other words, what is systemic is not a mistake and is done on purpose. Systematic is the process of becoming systemic. For example, when performed within a workplace environment, it involves procedures, routines, and an organizational culture that often contributes to less favorable outcomes for smaller groups of people and, therefore, in favor of the majority of its population by how their policies and programs are implemented.

Additional similar meanings for systemic include fundamental, integral, intrinsic, essential, innate, elemental, and ingrained. Others include methodical, precise, orderly, analytical, organized, regular, ordered, efficient and systematic. Done within a culture, it is the systemic pattern of behaviors created through the messages people receive about what is valued, with those messages coming from 3 primary sources: behaviors, symbols, and systems. To shape culture, the messages have to be aligned with these 3 channels. So, systemic is something that is done according to a fixed plan in a thorough and efficient manner.

CHAPTER: 0

A STARTING POINT

(My Perspective)

This chapter will introduce and intertwine some personal and political pet peeves surrounding the accurate teaching of History, the birth of "Race," political parties, and planet politics. Occasionally, I will make suggestions and state opinions I feel can rectify, remedy, or resolve them. Several foundational ideas and themes introduced here will be reiterated and developed. Again, when discussing racial issues, I'm never stereotyping all the people of a race or ethnicity. As far as I'm concerned, we're all the "Human Race" and species known as Homo Sapiens-Sapiens.

It wasn't me who decided to ethnically distinguish and categorize human beings. In fact, historically, being called a "Race" or an "ethnic group" is a fairly recent construct set-up by the influential power structures of the 15th through 18th centuries, including the "Roman Catholic Church" and all of whom, in my opinion, developed them to propagate and justify subjugating a particular people for the purposes of enslavement. It was men like Francois Bernier and Johann Friedrich Blumenbach who began separating the "human" species into races and ethnicities.

Francois Bernier (1625-1688) was among the first men known to divide the human race into ethnicities. He separated the globe into four subgroups: the Europeans, the Far Easterners, the Negroes (Blacks) and the Lapps. (1) It was Johann Friedrich Blumenbach (1752-1840) whose listings separated the "human" species into 5 ethnicities. According to Blumenbach, the "Caucasian" race were the people from Europe, the Caucasus Mountain regions, Asia Minor, North Africa, and West Asia and collectively known as the "White" species. He labeled the people of east, central, and southern Asia origins with the unflattering title of the "Mongoloid" species. He categorized those from the Sub-Saharan regions of Alkebulan (Africa) as the "Aethiopian" species, the "American" species were the people of North, Central, and South America, and lastly, the "Malayan" species consisted of the people from Southeast Asia (2).

I felt a flaw in his listings was not recognizing the entire Akebulan (African) continent consisted of dark-skinned people. In my opinion, he was implying that Caucasians built the Pyramids. There were several other "anthropologists" of note to come along and eventually label the people of my heritage as "Negro," a word of Portuguese origin from which other foul derivatives spun, like "nigger," "nigga," and "niggra." But…

"To the victor goes the spoils" (3) is a commonly misquoted saying that insinuates the winners of great battles and wars get to "call the shots" and change the rules, thus having history viewed/skewed from their point of view. Today we understand history has been "Hellenized" or viewed from the perspective of the Greeks and Romans. So, the inscriptions and writings on the halls and walls of the great monuments in Kemet were Hellenized and called "Hieroglyphics," whereas the Kemetians (Hellenized as Egyptians) actually called their writings, the "Medu-Neter," or "Medu-Netchur," which translates to "Mother Nature." (4)

Alexandria, the city off the Northern coast of Alkebulan, was named for "Alexander the Great," whom I call Alexander "The Greek," "The Brutal," or at the very least, the "Conquer." Alexandria became home to the infamously renowned "Library of Alexandria," which at the time was said to have held the sum total of the "known" world's knowledge from Egypt (Kemet), Asia, Greece, and Rome. The fall of this library, containing some now forever lost to the world knowledge, began with Julius Caesar, Emperor of Rome, who initially burned it.

It was then subsequently pillaged and pilfered by leaders of other ruling dynasties that followed including the Christian and Islamic Kingdoms. Like Alexander, the Roman conqueror "Scipio," aka "Scipio the Great," brought in his armies into Northern Akebulan and re-conquered Alexandria, earning him the title "Africanus," thereby claiming, then renaming the continent "Africa," becoming the first person to my knowledge, outside my heritage to label the people of my heritage. It's the primary reason I chose NOT to call myself, or the people of my heritage from or on the continent "African." The Greeks and, more so, the Romans were known as the "Great Copiers." Their scribes were assigned to copy the literature of other cultures into the library. These conquering kingdoms were also known to routinely claim ancient knowledge as their own and affix it as contributions made by people from their culture. For example, there were few men in the annuals of world history whose brilliant minds were known to influence the rest of humanity. Leonardo da Vinci was one such person. However, thousands of years before his birth, "Imhotep" was born in ancient Kemet (Egypt), whose name was Hellenized and changed to "Asclepius." Further discussion of him is forthcoming in these writings. I feel Nikolai Tesla was the third such brilliant mind.

I learned via a Google search that the first "forcibly imported" people of my heritage brought to America called themselves "Aqui" and called their continent Akebulan or Alkebulan, Kemet, Kush/Cush, or Ethiopia. **With three of them being Countries, Kingdoms, and Empires and no country ever called Alkebulan/Akebulan, I therefore chose to call the continent Akebulan or Alkebulan, which I will use interchangeably. Hence, I choose to identify myself as an American of Alkebulan/Akebulan heritage via slavery.

This differs from our beloved former President Barack Obama, whose patriarchal lineage extends directly from Akebulan and matriarchal lineage from the Caucasus Mountains. There is no slavery in his lineage. We also know the European conquerors stumbled into the Caribbean Sea and renamed the islands the "West Indies." When the British and Dutch colonies first set foot on the shores of what they were to rename America and saw the dark-skinned native people, they renamed them "Indians," thinking they sailed to the land called India.

At that time, no battles had been fought on these shores. I feel they saw people they felt they could take advantage of. A people they considered uncultured and/or less intelligent. The Indigenous Natives weren't initially hostile. In fact, they were helpful and lifesaving (hence, the first Thanksgiving). Some people seek to exploit weakness (like on the Alkebulan continent). To the colonialists, the Natives were seen as a vulnerable people and chose to impose their "Imperialistic" will, but to their dismay, these Natives were difficult to enslave.

With it being their native territory, they also had certain battle advantages that stunted the ideas of the Imperialists enslaving them. The "Invaders" eventually took another route of suppression known as "Annihilation" for these Natives they nicknamed "Redskins." To further justify their imperialistic desires, they called them "Savages." According to our movie media, the Natives nicknamed the white man "Pale Face." Historically, looking back, who were the actual Savages?

With the blessings of the Roman Catholic Church, the Portuguese began their trade of "Africans" in 1526 to South America, with the British and the Dutch to "America" initiating colonies "officially" in 1619, bringing enslaved people and indentured servants to the shores of what was to become the United States. What I'm saying is, since their claim of "Manifest Destiny," along with bringing the forcibly imported people of my heritage to these shores, there's constantly been this unrelenting practice of denying us our human and equal rights! In this case, I've included the Indigenous Native people, whose lands were totally confiscated. I ask, what gives you or anybody else the right to claim something belonging to someone else? We have a word for that. STEALING! In this instance, manifest destiny and stealing become synonyms.

It could be said that both the Akebulan and American continents were gangstered and stolen! I'm also reminded of eminent domain. I have a clearer understanding as to why the words to the "National Anthem" were adopted and why many are now calling for it to be revisited, reviewed, or outright rejected and rewritten. Its subliminal message is revolting, out of touch, and outdated. I agree it should be changed.

For example,

In verse 3, lines 5 & 6, it reads: No refuge could save the hireling and slave from the terror of flight or gloom of the grave.

In verse 4, lines 4, 5, & 6: Praise to the power that hath made and preserved us a nation.

Then conquer we must, when ours is just.

And this be our motto, In God is our trust.

I'm left to wonder, what god were they talking about? They sound a lot like today's white Christian Nationalists because it doesn't sound like the God of the Bible or of the "Golden Rule." I would suggest replacing the National Anthem with "Lift Every Voice And Sing" or writing a new one.

Today, I hear some white folk say, "You can't hold me responsible for what my ancestors did during the centuries of enslavement," and that's fair. I'm not holding you responsible for their transgressions against humanity; however, you are benefitting. I will connect some dots from what they did to what's going on today and purport there has never been a cessation of inequalities or intimidation in this country to date. In other words, the tyranny hasn't stopped, and I invite anyone to tell me when it did, a point I'll continually develop throughout the book by connecting dots to something else to demonstrate its unending morphing manifestations throughout America's historical timeline.

(Maga or Maggot)

The "MAGGOT" camp, I mean "MAGA" camp led by Donald Skunk, used that acronym to state, "Make America Great Again." I say you can't show me a period in our history that America has truly been great for all her people, particularly to her native and forcibly imported populations, which also refutes the statement that America is the land of immigrants. I'm certain Dr. Martin Luther King Jr would agree were he alive today.

There have been brief periods where conditions improved, followed by responding periods of crushing setbacks. So, possibly, we can say, "MABA" or "Make America Better Again." As I sat writing about the MAGA camp, I obviously was trying to be funny when I wrote MAGGOT. Then I thought, why not come up with an acronym for that? And I quickly came up with "Most Arrogant Garbage Got Overwhelmed Together."

In the Prelude, I referred to my inspiration(s) for writing this book, with one being the campaign and then the election of former president Donald Skunk (although I actually began writing in October 2021 and finished in October 2022). I also stated common sense ain't common these days. In 2016, I regularly rehearsed with 3 groups at my house. On one of our regular after-rehearsal discussions with one particular group, I told a couple guys I renamed each political party according to my reasoned observational assessment. Not trying to be offensive, the Republican Party "originally" became the "Repussican" (Re-pussy-can) Party.

My thinking was because, like pussy, they're more resilient and flexible, and collectively, right or wrong, they stick together better. And although I shared this with many women, recently one lady felt, in this case, my humor could be deemed disrespectful to women. So after thinking about it a little bit and not wanting to be disrespectful to the fairer sex and also because I didn't want to associate something so good with something so bad, I quickly came up with another pun and quickly renamed them the "Repunkian" (Re-punky-an) Party because I saw them more as "Chumps" or "Punks."

And like their symbolic elephant, which is known for its memory, they don't forget or forgive anything and will hold it against you. {Psalms 2:1-3 Why do the nations rage, And the people plot a vain thing? The Kings of the earth set themselves, And the rulers take counsel together…, saying, Let us break Their bonds into pieces And cast away Their cords from us.}

Repunkians reveal themselves to be unfair hypocrites who will "change the game in the game." For example, look how they "stuck together" with "Ditch Bitch" Mitch McConnell in denying former President Obama's selection of Merrick Garland to the Supreme Court. Here, McConnell lied and "made up" a rule stating the incumbent President couldn't make a selection to the Supreme Court within the last year of his administration. No such rule actually existed. The "Repunkian" Senate stuck together in the lie.

Remember, the Judge position became available on 2/13/2016 with roughly 11 months left in the Obama Administration. McConnell influenced and conveniently changed the "non-constitutional" Senate-created self-imposed filibuster rule's supermajority of 60 votes back to the regular "constitutional" simple majority and forced three extremely conservative judges onto the bench, with the last judge being confirmed within 6 weeks of Donald Skunk's Administration ending. A clear example of hypocrisy and "change the game in the game." Today's court would be 5-4 as opposed to 6-3 conservative.

They also used their wishy-washy filibuster to block important legitimate legislation, like John Lewis' voting rights bill, from coming to the Senate floor for a vote while simultaneously creating voter restrictive laws in their State Legislatures, including gerrymandering, like in North Carolina, where they gerrymandered the campus of HBCU University of North Carolina A & T that eliminated their "Black" Representative and created two "White" ones. Repunkians "stuck together" and passed Donald $kunk's tax cut to the wealthiest 3% of the population that grossly inflated the national debt by 7.8 trillion dollars while neglecting and ignoring the reality and existential threat to our planet of "Global Warming." That's some kind of sticking together when you're prepared to commit mass "global" suicide.

The Democratic Party earned two interchangeable names: The "Dimasscraps" (Dim-ass-crap) or "Dumasscraps" (Dum-ass-crap) Party because they often act as if they're stubborn, dim-witted, and slow to the game or just plain politically "Dum," as their symbolic Donkey represents. They often don't know when to stick together. For instance, after gaining back the majority, they were unable to demonstrate enough political savvy and collective cohesion to save "American Democracy" and get the same aforementioned (John Lewis) piece of voting rights legislation passed or balance the hypocritical imbalance on the Supreme Court created by Mitch McConnell, or stick together enough to save the planet.

They often appear "Dim" in their inability to, for example, adjust the Senate filibuster rule they also participated in creating that would at least permit legislation to be heard with the possibility of being considered for a vote. I feel you've reached the epitome of "dumbness," or call it stupidity if you know some group of people are willing to commit "mass climate suicide," and you allow them to kill you as well. Duh!

Then you have the Independent Party, whom I call the "Indepenis" (In-da-penis) Party. They have a tendency to independently "screw" everybody over. For example, when they chose to vote for the "greater" of two evils, as opposed to the "lesser." They invested their collective political stock and voted in Donald Skunk over Hillary Clinton. I'm not saying she was perfect, just clearly the lesser of two evils. They're also permitting State Legislatures to independently enact voter restrictive laws and making allowance for Global warming.

Finally, the Libertarian Party, whom I call "the Limitarian" (Limit-tarian) Party like "Grandstander" Rand Paul, a Senator from Kentucky who caucuses and votes with the "Repunkian" Party. They "usually" stand for the personal and civil liberties and freedoms afforded the People by the Constitution, (now seemingly only when it suits their outlook). I have to question his (their) stance on the Liberty suppressing policies espoused by the Repunkians, like abortion and voting rights restrictions or the "Stop and Frisk" policy that primarily affected the men of my heritage, who are routinely stopped and harassed by those sworn to "Serve and Protect," which often leads to unnecessary arrests/incarcerations and/or death.

What about the freedom and liberty to accurately teach the truth of our history or a COVID-19 vaccination shot and the wearing of masks? We knew before the pandemic that surgical masks have certain limitations. However, I have a statement for those refusing to wear them. Remind the surgical team to remove their masks on the next surgical procedure performed on you or a loved one! The "Limitarians" seem to "limit" the issues they speak up for.

Before I move on, I want to clarify my position on abortion. Yes, as common to most people, I feel there are things that are clearly wrong in this "civilized" world with some being worse than others. With that, "Man" has created a judicial system with laws that are pretty much universal around the globe. And as a Christian, I feel that God *giveth* and *taketh* away life. However, it is God who also gave mankind the free moral agency to make choices for ourselves and, thus, live with the consequences. Therefore, if God gives us the freedom to make our own choice on any given thing, whether good or bad, right or wrong, then what do I look like trying to limit anyone else's freedom to make decisions for themselves?

I thought to come up with my own political party concept, although I'm not promoting the actualization of the LPDCR or the LCDRP Party. The LPDCR or the Liberal Progressive Democratic Conservative Republic Party which means I'm for "Liberal" and "Progressive" ideas to sustain and grow our "Democracy" and upgrade our quality of life and to not squander or waste but "Conserve" the available resources at our disposal for the betterment of our "Republic." I also thought of the LCDRP Party, having the letters meaning, "Liberal" ideas to "Conserve" our "Democracy" and "Republic" as we "Progress" as a nation. My use of the word "liberal" in these examples means a wide variety.

To the American people of all political persuasions, I ask why anyone would choose to move backward to something that was obviously flawed as opposed to moving forward towards something new and improved, especially when you can clearly see Repunkians unilaterally opposing policies you often prefer. For example, the "ACA," aka "Obamacare?" The Repunkians blatantly lied to the public, for example, regarding "death panels."

American people of the Republican party, are you telling me when it comes to policies you favor, you'd rather go without because it was introduced by a Democrat, Independent, or Libertarian, especially when sometimes there isn't a single Repunkian willing to stand for what you desire? If so, you'd be willing to "cut off your nose to spite your face."

Today I feel people "choose" to be ignorant in our society because we live in the "information age." There's little excuse for anyone to be uninformed. However, we chose "not" to view all sides of an issue by "not" examining a variety of news sources. Every judge knows there are two sides to a story.

I've come to believe there's only one side, the truth! Anything else is just that, a story, a fabrication, or a lie. When I was born, there were 3 major news networks, ABC, CBS, and NBC. Their reporting of the news was consistent across the board, along with the published newspapers and news magazines, because they had to report facts and publicly retract anything that was incorrect because they could be sued.

Since the advent of "Social Media," you have people who are ignorantly equating it with the "News Media." However, we "expect" adults to understand the difference between the two, in that people can place an individual opinion on social media that, unfortunately, some folk "ASSUME" to be true. Have you heard the saying about what happens when you ASSUME; you make an (ASS of U & ME)." If mature adults are unable to discern this difference, then we have the blind leading the blind, which makes me question what parents are teaching their children.

I assert logic and reason dictates that "opinions" stated on social media can be based on a "purposeful lie," which often is the case (Donald Skunk's activity). Social media platforms "can" monitor posts placed on their platforms but "can't" be sued for the "opinions" expressed on them. Therefore, they're not held to the accountability imposed on the traditional published press and network broadcasts. Remember, I did mention the lack of common sense earlier.

(No Planet, No Peace)

A question I asked my musical comrades in January of 2016 was what they thought to be the single most important issue confronting humanity. One replied, "Pollution," and the other said, "Poverty," the two big P's. I agreed with their importance, but I dropped a third big P. I said it was the single issue that affected every living thing and without the third big P, the PLANET, we have nothing. I was referring to "Global Warming." I spoke of how, from my childhood, I had noticed the frequency and increased intensity of the weather patterns, both wet and dry, and how meteorologists started going through the entire alphabet and into the Greek alphabet when naming hurricanes.

I told them that as a youngster, I was always drawn to TV documentaries discussing the health of the planet, its increased warming, and how it would affect global weather patterns with increased intensity, affecting the jet stream, bringing drought, warming the oceans and altering currents, the coral reefs and aquatic life. How deforestation in the Amazon and Congo regions affects the planet's ability to breathe and replenish cool fresh air. During those discussions, I was driving my second hybrid vehicle, and I had done an accounting of the amount of money I spent on gas during the course of a year. I asked them to guess my gasoline costs. They had no clue and estimated thousands of dollars more than what I spent. I revealed it was a grand total of $252. One of them commented he spent $75 a week filling up his SUV. In one month, he had spent more than I had in a year.

Then I said if people refused to buy gas-powered vehicles and insisted on electric and/or hybrids, I felt it would make an immediate positive impact on the environmental climate and also reduce the cost of buying them, although I recognize there's a problem with safely disposing of the lithium batteries. I also told them I had no visible increase to my electric bill, and the only reason I had paid $252 was because of the manufacturer's recommendation to expel the gas every 3 months to avoid engine oxidation problems to the motor.

I proclaimed that unless we immediately face these issues and counter the problems associated with climate change, history would look back at us and proclaim our stupidity. They'll wonder how we permitted the power structure to dictate our losing the most precious thing we all share. Then I touted the only way effective change will occur is if the young people around the world got actively involved with their governments realizing this would be their issue to live and deal with.

As with us older folk, our young people also have to be held accountable for their role in today's "climate killing." So young people here's an opportunity for you to "show up!"

I feel wealthy politicians don't really care if we exist in a world that resembles the conditions in movies like "Mad Max Beyond Thunderdome" or "Soylent Green," where the planet has become a vast desert, and the "poor" people fight over its scarce and dwindling resources. We seem to be heading towards that state of the planet.

There is no time left to delay or make excuses because, in my opinion, we've already passed the point of certain devastation to our planet for decades, if not centuries, if not millennia! We witness it every day now. There are plans to colonize Mars, and some act as if that's a viable alternative to living on Earth. It's not! How would life on a desert planet without oxygen, scarce resources and under a dome be better than living under the open fresh air of our planet's atmosphere? Sounds like "Mad Max" to me. My question is, how can we have any semblance of peace on the planet when people are struggling for the basic primary resources of clean air, soil, and water with the ability to raise crops and livestock?

Have you, like I, been presented with the question of what is the most important thing we need to live. Are you thinking of food or water? The actual answer is... (Drum roll please)... Air/breath. In my concluding statements that day, I said to my friends, "I feel 'Oil Barons' are the biggest losers. I'm surprised they don't have the quality of personnel around them with the vision, business savvy, and ethical sensitivity surrounding the issues of global warming and climate change to have suggested they invest their "barrels" of wealth into 'Green Energies,' companies, and technologies.

They could've easily compounded their unimaginably vast amounts of wealth and controlled all the components having to do with the infrastructure for building, maintaining, and sustaining the Industries of electric vehicles, solar, wind, and other renewable 'green' energies and grids, as well perform a good deed for our planet and its citizenry."

I ended that conversation by saying: Starting in America (but also worldwide), all the vested companies and businesses, industries, and institutions negatively affecting the climate should be swiftly phased out if they don't quickly implement vitally necessary effective changes. This would hold all the world's governmental legislatures accountable. I'd otherwise call them "Climate Criminals" or enemies of the planet and of continued human existence if they continue to produce, promote, subsidize, and espouse the continuous use of petroleum products by drilling and fracking the planet to death.

I realize this sounds pretty extreme. However, our current situation is extremely urgent! I equated the oil within the planet to the cartilage on our bones. Bone against bone causes arthritis, and rock against rock causes earthquake.

Again, without a healthy planet, how can we have a healthy life? Is it wrong to be health conscience towards our planet? Is it wise to use and use up the limited, irreplaceable, highly toxic and polluting resources of gas and oil this way? Could they be used in a wiser, more conservative way? Our planet is rebelling against us because we've mistreated it. It's a natural reaction with all living things, and Earth is a living thing. By contrast, Mars is not! The "Golden Rule" extends to more than just people. You can't continuously abuse something without expecting an equal and opposite reaction. It's called "Cause and Effect."

(Sketchy Possible Counters To Global Warming)

Earlier, I referenced the Repunkicans' Party's tendency to stick together, good or bad, right or wrong. I cited the example of their collective denial of climate change and their willingness to commit mass global suicide and take all of humanity down with them! I'm dumbfounded by how nearly an entire political party could deny the obvious science of global warming, made evident since mankind has entered the "Industrial Revolution" around 1850 or so.

We've all been around a person who just complains and rarely has anything good to say or solutions to offer. Some might think I'm that type of person. Although I'm stating my views on this subject, I'm also willing to offer up some possible solutions, excepting the fact they aren't perfect or could be rejected outright. Nevertheless, I'm willing to have them scrutinized, tweaked, or rejected if it leads to active, meaningful steps being taken to counter this existential threat to every living thing on our planet! (RSWS: 1, 2, 4, 5, 6 & 9)

As I observe weather patterns across the country, I see the Western region experiencing massive drought and literally burning up. The Gulf region and East Coast are experiencing more intense hurricanes, tornadoes, and flooding, with Hurricane Sandy slamming into Atlantic City and New York City in 2012 being a prime example.

I'm proposing a system of water transportation from oversaturated areas to arid regions. For example, in places where we get heavy snowfall, rather than push the snow away, it's not beyond our ability to create the infrastructure to scoop it up and load it into/onto eventually all electrically powered vehicles I call "Snow Vacuums" that can also filter (from certain debris) and melt the snow on the spot from streets and sidewalks, lawns and parks and wide-open fields and farmlands.

Then, it can be taken and filtered into some type of reservoir near the rail lines and, put in storage container cars and shipped to the areas of drought where it can be carefully released in the mountains or the natural tributaries and aquifers as if it were rainwater. Storage tanker cars on trains could also be fitted with wide funnels to capture snow and rain in strategically placed locations where heavy precipitation is expected to fall.

I've seen footage of huge chunks of ice breaking off glaciers and falling into the ocean. I heard about a dangerous rouge ice sheet, "Breaking Bad," off the Antarctic continental plate. Rather than allow it and other broken-off glaciers to just melt into the ocean and raise the overall water levels worldwide, why not capture them, break them into smaller chunks, put them on tanker ships, and melted as drinking water or used for irrigation or as I spoke of earlier in the US and in other needy places around the world?

Why should we let it go to waste? And since pipelines are used for moving oil and natural gas, couldn't we and other countries use pipelines for shipping this overflow of floodwaters from one region to another? Finally, I thought, why not take those used up Lithium batteries and place them back in the holes they were dug from? Again, I'm not claiming these to be perfected ideas, just starting platforms.

(Conspiracy Theories)

Most of us have entertained a conspiracy theory or two. After the 2020 election of President Joe Biden, Donald Skunk and company floated one, which he refers to as "The Big Lie." I've heard it said that if you tell a lie, tell a big lie! However, his conspiracy threatens to tear apart the country because his followers "choose not" to look at both sides of the story or view a variety of news sources, excluding social media, which is often not a news source. Had I started writing this book in January of 2016, to some, I may have looked like a prophet of sorts per the many conversations with my buddies, some of which I've also shared with you in this reading. Over the course of time, historically, "Big Lies" have done so much harm in the country and particularly to those sharing my heritage.

I ask you to please indulge me as I tap into a few conspiracy theories that I've considered. Again, one of my inspirations for writing this book was the election of former president Skunk. In another conversation with my previously mentioned friends, I asked them what they thought was the "worst thing" that then newly elected president Skunk could do to the country. One said he could take us into a war, and the other said he could ruin the economy. Again, I agreed with them both. But before I tell you how I replied, I'll briefly reflect on theirs.

Think back to October of 2019. Former president $kunk had the American people and the world holding our collective breath, thinking we were about to witness the start of World War III by going to war with Iran over the "Iran Nuclear Deal" that he exited from. He then elevated his rhetoric against Iran and brought the country to the brink of war. Regarding ruining the economy, he did an excellent job of that with his handling or mishandling of the COVID-19 virus crises.

We now know he also then withheld vital information from the American public of its seriousness, proper safety measures, and its' transmission and spread. The facts came out that during that time, he habitually lied and dispensed misinformation (Ex. His "The virus would be gone by April" statement and let us inject some bleach into our veins). His actions, or lack thereof, caused hundreds of thousands of lives to be unnecessarily lost, spawned the expansion of the virus and its subsequent variances, and, by extension, caused an extended shutdown of the country, resulting in its economic downturn and the loss of millions of jobs. Then he gifted the wealthiest 3% of our population a tax cut, which exploded the national debt more than any other president in a 4 year period.

When it came to my answer, I told my partners that I felt he would try and steal the country and we should have a militia in place to counter his intended dictatorship! I stated his previous media presence had never captured my attention, including his TV show and I only really became aware of him because of his comments referencing the birth of President Obama. I knew of but shared my vagueness about his comments regarding the "Bronx 5" at the time. I soon learned they erroneously served jail terms that were overturned because they were subsequently proven innocent, but "candidate" Donald Skunk still insisted these innocent young men of color be put to death. Soon after his ride down the escalator announcing his candidacy for the presidency came his Mexican drug dealing rhetoric.

Around the same time, I became aware of his and his family's historical track record with housing discrimination. As I observed his campaign rhetoric, I expressed my newly formed opinion of him and concluded he was a sociopathic psychopath, a callously unemotional and morally depraved individual unfit for the Presidency or anything else of consequence, as demonstrated by his rant against the physically handicapped reporter, his comments on "grabbing pussy" and busting in the dressing rooms of the young women during his Miss Universe contests in Russia and of his Russian financial connections and money laundering schemes, as well as by the violence he encouraged and directed towards a man of my heritage who spoke out in opposition against him at one of his campaign rallies.

He then proved my point on a daily basis throughout his time in the White House. I told my buddies I felt he was a "Manchurian Candidate" completely in the hands of Vladimir Putin and his cohorts. I also shared my conspiracy theory on the "pee pee" tape, which is so vulgar that I won't share it here. I told my buddies I felt the Repunkicans would go along with the program because Putin had already communicated with that party, promising some of them influential positions while threatening the lives of others in forming the new "DDA" or "Disunited Dictatorship of America." Then told them I felt Putin would renege on most of them and do to them as the popular Russian vodka "Popov" and "pop off" them or "pop them off" via assassinations if they refused to go along with the program. After all, Putin is a known former KGB official/agent and assassin.

I went on to say that Donald Skunk would saturate us with lies and nonsense to distract us from the truth, citing the analogy of, if I threw 10 hard fastballs at you at the same time, how many of them would catch? You'd be lucky to catch one. Look how many would get past you. That's exactly what he did to the American public. He threw so many fastballs at us that we literally couldn't keep up with his "Bu!!$#i+." Neither the network broadcast and cable news media nor the printed press were able to keep pace with him. They couldn't develop one of his scandalous storylines before the next outrageous comment or event came out, which was usually the next day. I told them when he lied on or pointed the finger at somebody, it was easy for him to do because it was something he had personally done and was already guilty of because it was part of his everyday lifestyle. I called it live reality TV. He was recorded and fact-checked as telling over 31,000 lies while in office. Doing a little math, that over 7,750 lies a year, which comes out to roughly 21 lies a day and nearly one lie per hour. I'll discuss this further in the last chapter.

(Remember the Tuskegee Institute's "Syphilis Study" and Henrietta Lacks)

I believe some people don't want "all" of American History taught because they might feel some level of guilt from the atrocities many of their ancestors committed against targeted segments of the population for reasons of greed and the hue of their skin. However, the people who share my heritage have some real viable and valid reasons to believe various conspiracy theories.

I'm not referring to his made-up notorious "BIG LIE" of the most secure, free, and fair election in this country's history, with its violence perpetuated by people choosing to be ignorant. American history is replete with examples of restrictive laws, both formal and informal, along with regulations, statutes, and court cases that conspired to restrict and deny the people of my heritage equitable opportunities socially, economically, educationally, and otherwise (RSWS: 1, 2, 3, 4, 5, 6, 7, 8, & 9). The Tuskegee Institute's Syphilis Study is a fact, not a conspiracy theory! (5)

The "Medical Science" community actually conspired and performed "secret" experiments under the guise of the people suffering from what was called "Bad Blood." Several ailments like diabetes, high blood pressure, and tuberculosis were considered and covered under the broad classification of "Bad Blood." For the test group in this covertly conducted study from 1932-1972, medical professionals recruited 600 poor and impoverished "African-American" men and sharecroppers in Macon County, Alabama, then "secretly" injected/infected 399 of them with the Syphilis virus without their consent or knowledge of the real intent of the study. To induce their participation in this appalling study, the men were promised free lifetime medical care (RSWS: 1, 5, 6, & 8).

These so-called "medical investigatory hypocrites," whom I call "fiendish mad scientists" synonymous with those of the Hitler camp, willingly broke their Hippocratic Oath and then observed and chronicled the progression of the three stages of this horribly degenerative disease as it overtook these men as they sadly and painfully died. These actions were extremely evil, cruel, immoral, simply wrong, and possibly demonic and/or satanic. I won't gloss over the seriousness of this and will highlight the 3 stages of its progression. I also wonder how many of these men unknowingly impregnated and infected other people (primarily women) and what ultimately was the totality of infected people in and outside that community.

Stage one begins with the appearance of painless sores around the genitals and mouth called "chancres." Although the sores would disappear within a few weeks, the glands around these areas usually became enlarged. The second stage involved feeling ill with headaches and fever. Rashes appeared on the body, often around the hands and feet. Other symptoms could include hair and weight loss. Both men and women would have noticed skin growths around their genitals, particularly around the anus. Women also experienced it around their vaginal regions. Remember, these women weren't provided any medical care because they weren't "officially" part of the study. The third or latent stage was without obvious symptoms. However, the syphilis caused serious damage to important organs, including the heart, brain, and nervous system, which would linger for years. (6)

At this stage, the Syphilis infection became fatal, resulting in death. No other people in this country were experimented on like that and like those placed in Nazi Germany internment camps (RSWS: 9). A much lesser known covertly conspiratorial study was performed on a woman of my heritage, also without her consent or knowledge, was the cancer study performed on "Ms. Henrietta Lacks." The use of her "Immortal Cells" are still being used in many of the advances being made in the curing of cancer today. She or her family has never been notified or received compensation (RSWS: 1, 5, & 8). A Google search will shed more light on the "secret research" performed on her. (7)

(The COVID-19 Virus)

After learning about the covert syphilis (studies) experiments, it's not surprising many people of my heritage are often skeptical or reluctant about receiving injections or inoculations of any kind. As a teacher, I never took a flu shot and never caught the flu in over 24 years of service. In the case of COVID-19, I did get the recommended shots and boosters, then contracted the virus within a month after taking the second booster. However, I showed no symptoms. I do have my own conspiracy theory regarding the virus as it relates to "pre-existing conditions."

My question is, how can you have a pre-existing condition for something that didn't exist until "presto, all of a sudden?" In other words, how can I have a pre-existing condition for something that doesn't (didn't) exist? I realize there is a branch of viral science given to creating and curing viruses, and for whatever reasons, discussions have circulated around the virus somehow being leaked from a Chinese laboratory. With the pre-existing conditions disproportionately affecting the people of my heritage, you can begin to understand why people might conclude this cooked concoction was a customized laboratory special. I'm reminded of the movie, "12 Monkeys," where it's portrayed how quickly a leaked virus could/would circumnavigate the planet.

During my senior year of college, I took a physical health course where I was tested for things like my body fat content, diabetes, and tuberculosis, and even how fast my first step was. I learned I had the quickest first step on campus, faster than all the athletes. I didn't know that a cholesterol test was administered. In fact, I wasn't aware of cholesterol at all. When I viewed the results, I thought nothing of it and don't recall there being any real discussion on cholesterol. I "assumed" all things were normal. After recently reviewing it, I saw that my cholesterol was 212. That was ridiculously high for a 21-year-old in the best shape of his life who really didn't eat that much and had already become an herbalist. Anything over 150 is high.

Born in 1960 and growing up in the 1970s, it was a time when television wasn't bombarded with "Big Pharma" commercials advertising and promoting medicines as they do today. I recall only 4 medicine commercials that stick out in my mind. Bayer Children Aspirin, Phillip's Milk of Magnesia, Pepto-Bismol, and Dristan. Dristan was most unique in that it was known for its "time-released medicine," which became the key element of my conspiracy theory tied in with inoculations and pre-existing conditions.

My mind began to percolate and circulate around the idea of what if at birth when you got your first inoculations, aka your "baby shots," that some "rogue" medical professionals decided to inoculate the people of my heritage with a "time-released" drugs that would make us susceptible to a variety of illnesses, particularly the ones considered pre-existing conditions to COVID-19, which are diabetes, high blood pressure, and elevated cholesterol.

Sounds pretty far-fetched, huh? Well, it's now known that the futuristic technologies we see at the movies and on TV are some 20 to 30 years or more in production ahead of being released and known to the public! As a child I regularly visited the Museum of Science and Industry, where I witnessed

"Zoom" technologies at the time. If you watch "Star Trek," the original series, they used the technology then, as well as "the communicator," aka the "flip phone." Today, many of those 1960s technologies are commonplace around the world. How long did it take before their introduction back then that they became commonplace today? Bear with me as I present a couple more thoughts and feelings on conspiracies.

(The "Co-Intel" Program)

The "Counterintelligence Program" or "Co-Intel Program" was covertly initiated and enforced by said to be a "black" man," J Edgar Hoover, first Director of the FBI. I've Googled information that traces his ancestral lineage back into enslavement. Hoover was also reported to be a "closet" homosexual as it was called back then, thus earning the nickname "Gay Edgar Hoover," a nickname I've heard several people call him. Today, with the exception of some Repunkican politicians, fortunately, there's little to no stigma attached to one's sexuality and, therefore, no need to be "in the closet." However, Hoover was known to blackmail people for any dirt he was able to dig up on them, so I felt he was a hypocrite!

I personally don't have any issue with a person being of the LGBTQ+ community. From my childhood, I've had gay friends and family associates when it was stigmatized. My pet peeve is when someone shares their sexual preference upon being introduced. That's personal business and, in some cases, obvious, but when it's not, I still prefer we get to know each other better before revealing such intimate details. The Principal at the last High School I taught did just that when she introduced herself to the school's teaching staff the week before classes started. She stated her name and then said, "And I'm a lesbian," in that order. I felt it was a little too personal too soon and found it offensive. During the course of that day, I found myself thinking, what did her sexual preference have to do with our instruction of the students.

On the other hand, if I, meeting you for the first time, said, "Hello, my name is _____, and I'm heterosexual" or "and I'm NOT gay," I'm sure it would create an awkward moment. At the end of the year, after the students were dismissed for summer vacation and on the very last day of school of a three-day session that concluded with teachers' meetings, I wore a t-shirt purchased in the Bahamas that was labeled FBI, which clearly stated "Female Body Inspector." It wasn't intended to be the stupid, insensitive, sexist act it was, and I was simply a numbskull. However, when I checked my mailbox at the end of the day, there was a letter of reprimand from guess who, the principal herself.

Hoover, with his spying Co-Intel Program, kept secret files on government officials, politicians, and powerful people in industry, the media, the ministry, educational institutions, and private citizens, using it as a means of blackmail and control. He was known to target and then infiltrate organizations with "plants" to keep track of their planned activities. The "Historically Black Colleges and Universities aka "HBCU's," were one such institution. He was said to have kept files on the Student Government Presidents as "potential or future Leadership." Gaining knowledge of this information left me with a level of anxiety and a bit paranoid because I served as a "Student Government President" at one of 11 in the state of North Carolina, which hosts more than any other State (RSWS: 1, 2, 4, 5, & 6).

I'll only scratch the surface on this one final theory I chose to list. I would say most of us recognize the controlled demolition of a building upon viewing. I'm referring to the September 11, 2001 event, aka "9/11," where 3 of the 7 buildings at the World Trade Center complex in New York City came crashing down like a controlled demolition after "terrorist" commandeered airplanes and slammed them into the "Twin Towers" and the Pentagon. Building 5, which I wasn't aware of at the time, had fallen later the same day. This building of 48 floors was never touched by a plane and had only a small fire but came crashing down classic controlled demolition style as well.

It also happened to house gold reserves. Like most people old enough to remember, I was teaching in my music class, which was the only class that always had a TV available to it because it occupied the entire 4th floor (which was inaccessible to a service elevator). After learning the first plane crashed into the tower, my television was on for the remainder of the day. My classes witnessed the 2nd plane crash into the 2nd tower, and both towers fell. My immediate and initial thought was those buildings came neatly crashing down like a controlled demolition!

I later learned plausible information explaining what caused the Twin Towers to collapse, but none of that information was applicable to Building #5. What I do know is other skyscrapers taller than 48 floors have caught fire and burned for much longer periods. Some of them burned for days, but all of them are still standing today. The fact that jet fuel burns around 1,517 degrees and steel beams begin to be compromised between 2,550-2,777 degrees was also inconsistent for building #5 because no jet ever touched it. However, regarding the towers collapsing, I was shown how to fold the $5, $10, $20, $50, and the $100 bills in the same precise order, revealing the Twin Towers standing untouched on the $5 bill, both buildings smoldering on the $10, the first Tower falling on the $20 bill, the second building fallen in a cloud of dust on the $50, then finally on the $100 bill, both buildings fallen, left in a wisp of smoke. I actually have the picture of the folded money in one of my old phone's photo gallery. Two noted DVDs from that era are "Fahrenheit 911" and "In Plane Sight."

I later witnessed on the news coverage, as nearly everyone else, how former President George "Dummy" Bush reacted after he learned of the first plane striking the initial Tower when a presidential aid whispered in his ear, and how he first sat speechless and looked dumbstruck before he started reading to the class again, rather than immediately leaving that classroom and act on behalf of the country. In his defense, I heard him say many years later in a documentary that a President's first job is to present calm.

I also learned through my DVD collection that there was a very close relationship with the then Saudi Arabian Ambassador to the United States, Prince Bandar (Bin Laden) Sultan (cousin to Osama Bin Laden), and President Bush. It was reported that they were so close that Bush nicknamed him "Bandar Bush." Like me, Bush is known to nickname people. For example, he nicknamed his then Secretary of State Condoleezza Rice "Condy." Last but not least, Melvin Bush, the younger brother of President Bush, ended his tenure as "Head of Security" for the World Trade Center complex on September 10, 2001, one day before the terrorist attack. Was that coincidence merely luck?

With that, I'll leave the surface scratched (RSWS: 1, 5, 6, & 9).

(Teaching History aka CRT; You Can't Blame Me For What My Ancestors Did)

Banning books! What gives anyone the right to ban my (our) 1st Amendment right of freedom of speech…to talk, teach, read, or write about history or anything else for that matter? I agree and accept some things should be rated "X" or "PG" (Parental Guidance), where parents have the decided say so over what, when, and how some information is disseminated to their children. However, upon the age of consent, it becomes the child's individual choice.

We all have the right to learn or teach about history, even if some others don't want to teach or learn about "actual" history. For example, you have people making like America's beginnings were so "great" for its native and forcibly imported enslaved populations. Will banning "Black History Month" be next on the CRT haters' "cancel culture" agenda because they've decided to water history down, then say we can't discuss our own history in this country because these truths make "them" feel uncomfortable.

History is exactly what it is and can't be chosen and picked over like vegetables at a grocery store. I spoke earlier of history being "Hellenized" with some facts historically altered. Shall we say the current version of history is "Americanized?" Remember the famous line from the movie "A Few Good Men": "You can't handle the truth!" History doesn't teach us to "hate ourselves," it teaches us to reflect on our deeds in an honest, open, and realistic manner and, when to recognize and be disgusted with the deplorable acts of our past, and to act on it for the betterment of civilization.

The only way you would hate yourself today is if you, as a seasoned adult, have a significant track record of atrocities and/or are currently committing deplorable acts against others and realize your actions will be viewed as a part of tomorrow's history. There should never be any or debate whether or not to teach US history any other history. It should be taught accurately, honestly, and truthfully. It would be a ludicrous lie not to!

However, some people still say no to the truth! They seem to want the ostrich version of history taught where you bury your head in the sand and, for example, not teach the horrific truths of slavery as being one of America's original sins. I raise this question. Should this and other sad or uncomfortable facts of American History be known or buried? Remember, "The devil is a liar, and the truth is not in him." More on that biblical verse later.

Beginning early on the morning of September 17, 1862, during the Civil War, Confederate and Union troops clashed near Maryland's Antietam Creek. It was the bloodiest single day of battle in American military history. This American historical fact evaded some of the smartest people in the country when the panel of three (white people in this case) appeared on "Jeopardy" in April 2022. I watched the episode. I was also ignorant of this fact because it's not drilled into our heads like the overhyped fable of George Washington and the Cherry tree. Shall we follow his admonition and not "lie" to ourselves!

Today, teaching history is often "radicalized" and marginalized, as with so many other important issues facing this country and the world. Today's media often packages issues into words and catchphrases like "cancel culture" and "1619 Critical Race Theory," aka "CRT." The "original enslaving settling invaders" neatly packaged their propaganda, calling the people of my heritage "chattel" and labeling the indigenous peoples as "savages." This made it easier for them to justify and then execute a campaign of murdering and corralling them to mostly unproductive areas they called "reservations." At the same time, they were stealing their lands from underneath them, claiming "Manifest Destiny."

Well, I have "reservations" about not teaching these truths. On the contrary, Native populations have shown themselves to be some of the most peaceful, nature-loving people on the planet. What would you do if someone came to your house, ravaged it, then took it from you?

Manifest Destiny is defined as the idea that the United States is destined by "God" to expand its Dominion and spread democracy and capitalism to the entire North American Continent. That's "STEALING," which is defined as taking (another's property) without permission or legal right and without intending to return it. That makes Manifest Destiny and stealing synonyms. This lines up with "eminent domain" and also "redlining" (RSWS: 1, 4, 5, 6, 7 & 9). Looking at the systematic intent of "manifest destiny" along with the systems of eminent domain and redlining in yesterday's and today's housing discrimination implementations, for example, demonstrates something that has become "systemic" in this country.

(Radical Rascals)

To radicalize something means to thoroughly change it as it relates to affecting the fundamental nature of it. In other words, it's been over-exaggerated and made into a lie. The actual teaching of History is not the teaching of lies but the teaching of the truths. To say teaching "CRT" is teaching all of American History would be an exaggerated and "radicalized" version of it. "CRT" is "ONLY A PART" of our story as a country. BUT MAKE NO MISTAKE ABOUT IT… IT'S DEFINITELY A PART OF IT and should be taught as well!

To accurately teach American history means truthfully teaching the fact that slavery and the resulting racial discrimination are a part of our American story and journey. Otherwise, it's not the truth of "History." It would be a fable or a story, aka "fiction," which is something made up! To change a story of this magnitude would be known not as history but as "HIS STORY!"

For instance, a simple Google search reveals that the history or rather the fable that Christopher Columbus "discovered America" is an example of a "Big Lie" that integrated itself into the fabric of this country's "His Story" and not our history! It's an example of History being rewritten and idealized. Remember the quote that has been brain-ingrained into the national DNA through the educational system, "In 1492, Columbus sailed the ocean blue. He had three ships and sailed from Spain." "The Nina, the Pinta, and the Santa Maria" roll off our tongues almost automatically.

When, in fact, we know he was in search of an alternate and shorter route to Asia, specifically India. That's the extent of the truth! He never set foot on the shores of what we call "America," aka the "USA," and yet he was honored with monuments and a national holiday every 2nd Monday in October that only recently changed in the last few years.

When you Google Search the "Voyages of Columbus," it reveals that his early voyages took him first to an island called by the native Lucayan people as "Guanahani" known today as the Bahamas. I happened to be there during their acknowledgment of the 500th year of his voyage to their shores. I chose the word "acknowledgment" rather than celebration as a personal choice. He then subsequently visited the islands known as Cuba and Hispaniola where Haiti eventually was birthed, and where he established a colony that later became the country "The Dominican Republic." In his later two voyages, he traveled to eastern Central America and northern South America. What is not taught and memorialized are the sufferings, trauma, and pain that he and his fellow explorers and crews inflicted upon the Indigenous populations as they enslaved, murdered, and raped them during the assimilation process.

Something I was aware of that the Google search also revealed is that it was Amerigo Vespucci (1451or1454-1512), an enslaving practitioner and contemporary of Columbus, who actually determined that he landed on a "New" continent, now Rio de Janeiro, Rio de La Plata and Cape Verde, South America and not Asia (India) and that the American Continent was actually named for him by way of some German using a Latinized feminine version of his first name. Question, why didn't they call the new land "Vespuccia" or "Ameriga?" Is it because the letters of "AMERICA," which reconstituted, spell out: "I AM RACE?"

(Sticks And Stones May Break My Bones…)

It's universally understood that those who are ignorant of the former historical track record are more likely to repeat similar acts and errors and therefore retarding progress. Some act as if progress or being "progressive" is a bad thing. In my opinion, that would be an example of a closed-minded person. An understanding of our past record reveals things we have done well and things we've executed poorly. We can profit from this record both by building upon our strengths and by deconstructing our failures, then building back better from them. The general idea is to progress and to make things better for our civilization, species, and world. The key part of the word civilization is "civil," indicating things should be done equitably, fairly, and justly for everyone.

The saying, "Sticks and stones may break my bones, but words can never hurt me," is a major misnomer. Sticks and stones definitely can inflict bodily injury, and likewise, some words can scar your soul, emotions, and spirit. The biblical verse of Proverbs 22:6 states, "Train up a child in the way he should go, and when he is old, he will not depart from it." Few are able to break that cycle.

So I ask, by your example, do you train your children to call people stupid, nigger or white trash etc…? Are you teaching truths or lies with your words and actions? Some white folk say, "You can't hold me responsible for what my ancestors did," but do you teach or deny the fact that your ancestors' actions do directly affect the people of my heritage today, or do you just avoid the subject?

"They" should've been held accountable for their actions of yesteryear (but they weren't), just as you are responsible for your actions TODAY because some of you are the "They" today! I'm referring to those who chose to lie or deny the truth in an attempt to, for example, rewrite the history of the January 6 insurrection. Today, for those sharing my heritage, words like "excessive police violence" and "unnecessary shootings," or "qualified immunity" can be rather painful.

Some words seem to grab my attention and foster my desire to understand them on a deeper level. For example, the word "nice" fosters a good feeling within us. I've been called nice often, and perhaps you have been also. However, after researching it, I learned it's an old French word referring to the city of "Nice," which originally meant stupid, ignorant, and incapable. Now I understand the phrase, "Nice guys finish last." I tell people today, don't call me a nice guy. You can call me a good man or a decent person.

There's another word that has recently come into our cultural vernacular. Before revealing it, I want to describe it and give you an either-or choice in determining whether it's a word you'd call yourself. Would you describe yourself as discouraged or dissuaded, tired like, or in a constant mental fog? Or would you describe yourself as stirred up, aroused and aware, animated or lively? If you decided you were the second description, you chose some synonyms of the word "Woke." If you're not "woke," you obviously must be… what Asleep!

What's your preference? Some politicians have chosen NOT to be "woke" but asleep on the job of handling our country's affairs. Are you sleeping on your watch, too? Personally, I'd rather be "woke" so that I can get information and decide what to do with it, rather than dreaming or daydreaming my way through life. It's your choice whether you consciously make it or not!

Some words like systemic racism are painful, and group names like the Ku Klux Klan, the "Alt-Right" or white "Christian" nationalist, Neo-Nazi, the Proud Boys, The Three Percenters, The Minute Men, and the little-known but cleverly dressed up, "Identity Europa" aka The American Identity Movement (AIM) "literally" hurt people. "They" evoke fear, terror, and strife. We all have to look at ourselves in the mirror. Tell me, what do YOU see looking back at you? By implication, "They" feel their lives and opinions are most important and fundamental to "our" country.

Is this why so much ire is evoked towards the "Black Lives Matter" movement? Today, their comeback is "All" lives matter. However, you've never said or acted like that during the course of our national history. This is hypocrisy and having your cake and eating it to. You don't want to share it! You're like a horse with blinders on. The gall of that level of blatant hypocrisy is mind-boggling!

Who are the "They" today? I'm referring, in the broader sense, to the Repunkican Party, not true Republicans. To narrow it down, it's the MAGA or MAGGOT-spouting people of the groups I just listed. "They" are a wimpy bunch of crybabies when "They" don't get their way. And to "They" who say you can't blame me for what my ancestors did during slavery, well, it looks to me like "Somebody" is trying to re-enslave people today through politics, poverty, education, and incarceration. That "Somebody" is the "They" of today. Is that an example of "MAGA" when "their" leader spouts off at his rallies of how people opposing his ideas and opinions should or would've been beaten like "in the good 'ole days?" Is that what "They" call making America great again?

Finally, I hold your great, great, great grandparents accountable for what "They" did. You know, the ones practicing "slavery" and Native American annihilation. Then later, it was your great-great-grandparents for the dismantling of the Reconstruction Era and allowing for the setting up of the first domestic terrorist groups like the Ku Klux Klan and the "White Leagues," and for setting up sharecropping, the "Black Codes," and permitting countless senseless lynching.

I hold your great grandparents accountable for maintaining "Jim Crow" through the institutionalized segregation of "Separate but Equal" and the continued lynching, "Drowned Towns," land grabs, and the burnouts of Tulsa, Oklahoma, Rosewood, Florida, etc.… I hold your grandparents accountable for the continued segregation of housing discrimination, redlining, and Emmet Till and the violent protests against civil rights marchers, attack dogs, and murdering Dr. Martin Luther King, Medgar Evers, and The Black Panther Party, etc.… I hold you and your parents to account for people like Kyle Rittenhouse, the death of George Floyd, Ahmaud Arbery, and today's voter restricting gerrymandering of State districts and the insurrection on our US Capitol in Washington DC, just to reveal the tip of the iceberg.

So, where is this "greatness" that America can go back to and be made great again? I reiterate I'm not talking about all the white folk in the country! This only applies to a growing number of the "They." It's the ones who are offended by 1619 CRT or this book. It's the same people who pledged allegiance to the Confederate flag on "insurrectionist day" and who felt the need for a violent overthrow of our country when the election didn't go "their" way.

You can try and justify your actions, but you can't truly lie to yourself or to most people in this country and you certainly can't lie to me! Consider this, if the 2020 election had been rigged, common sense dictates the Dimasscraps would've overwhelmingly been elected and ruling the House of Representatives, the Senate and State legislatures around the country. They barely have majorities in the House, and the Senate is 50/50 as of this writing.

It turns out that only members of the Repunkican party and the Skunk Administration attempted to rig the elections by attempting to implement "the fix" by way of gerrymandering their State legislatures and imposing alternate electoral slates. I can't recognize any viable positive legislative policy from them, only lies, conspiracies, and misdirection.

If you look at the history of violence directed towards governmental institutions in this country, the groups that have been violently mistreated, the Indigenous Natives, and people sharing my heritage have historically been the least anti-governmental. Our protests, with a few exceptions, have primarily been in the form peaceful marches, while chanting or singing songs of weariness and hope for a better day.

Recently, however, there have been alleged acts of violence in some "Black Lives Matter" demonstrations. I'll temper this with two facts. First, it accounts for less than 3% of the violence of any and all protests in the country, and second, I wouldn't dismiss the possibility that some participants were purposely placed there as "plants" to initiate violence. I imply this because usually our protests are multiracial, unlike the alt-right/Neo Nazis protest in Charlottesville, Virginia, for example, or basically the groups who stormed and busted up the US Capitol building while attempting to purposefully overthrow a free and, most notably, the fairest election in American history. I would be willing to wager that a fair amount of the violent protesters in Charlottesville were also present at the US Capitol on "Insurrectionist Day," January 6, 2021.

If you are opening this book and starting your reading here, then you're not starting at the beginning. In fact, you are well into the book. I ask you to return to the "FOREWORDS" and begin reading. Otherwise, you won't have a clear perspective of my points of view, and much of what you read could be taken out of context. Also, the book ends with the last word of the AFTERWORDS section

Chapter: 1

WHEN YOU POINT THE FINGER AT SOMEONE, YOU'VE GOT THREE FINGERS POINTING BACK AT YOU...

(Divide And Conquer)

...And, as some would say, with one pointing up at God. It's easy for us to identify the flaws and faults in others, but we often find it more difficult to identify our own. Outside the occasional demented psychopath or sociopath, I think we humans tend to believe we're decent people trying to do the right things for ourselves, our families, and our friends within our communities. Most of us are basically balanced thinkers and acknowledge we have faults and have likely said, "I know I'm not perfect."

However, if asked to identify your own faults, you might find it difficult after identifying a couple obvious ones. We tend to strive for perfection in our pursuits. I compare it to a pitcher in Major League Baseball who, with every opportunity given, pitches not only to win and complete the game but seeks to pitch a no-hitter or, more so, pitch the "perfect game." That happens when no batter on the opposing team gets to first base. Most "God-fearing people" seek a perfection that can only ultimately be achieved upon being received into the Kingdom of God.

While speaking for myself, I feel nobody likes being criticized and don't usually invite constructive criticism either. I think we try to do things perfectly while realizing we're not, but deep down wishing we were. We've all come across that person we feel, "They think they're perfect." It's a vibe they send out, the "Mr. Know-It-All" type or "I'm never wrong about anything."You or I could observe that person and likely identify a number of their faults, starting with self-righteousness. Since I'm going to be pointing out many injustices directed towards the people of my heritage and pointing the finger at those I feel are historically responsible, I think it's only fair to point out some flaws I've observed within my own community. I'll point the 3 fingers back at me, or the collective we, so to speak.

(The Slave Trade)

With the blessings and sanctions of the Roman Catholic Church in 1526, the "official" slave trade began its three-legged triangular route, with Spain and Portugal leading the way (RSWS: 1, 4, 5, 6, 7 & 8). Books like The Atlantic Slave Trade by Billy Wellman, The Transatlantic Slave Trade (overcoming the 500-year Legacy by Benjamin F. Chavis Jr, and The Slave Trade (The Story of the Atlantic Slave Trade:1440-1870) by Hugh Thomas provide deeper insights into this deeply disturbing topic. But for the purposes of this reading, I will abbreviate and condense the information to be easily digestible.

With that being said, the European Atlantic slave trading nations listed in order according to their trade volume were Portugal, Britain, Spain, France, the Dutch, and the Danish. Many of them had established outposts, with the 2nd point and 1st leg of the triangular trip, to the Alkebulan or "African" West Coast, where they then traded for slaves with local leadership (a point that's been disputed, in that some say those leaders were initially forced into those dealings because of guns vs spears).

Companies like the infamous Dutch East India Company were established to provide cargo protections for ships sailing from Europe with their manufactured goods to the West coast of Akebulan from Liberia to Nigeria.

They then traded over weeks and months for the captured people provided by Alkebulan traders. From there, the captured enchained people would literally be shipped to the 3rd point and 2nd leg of the triangle, to the Americas and the islands in the Caribbean Sea, aka, the "Middle Passage." After unloading their enchained cargo, the ships would begin the 3rd leg of the voyage by returning to the first point of the triangle, back to Europe.

Slavery has occurred throughout all of mankind's existence. However, the colonies established in what became the USA were historically the worst and demonstrated the cruelest, most brutally violent form of slavery known to man. Although still inhumane, cruel, and unfair, the other forms of enslavement in the Americas and Caribbean Sea paled by comparison to that of the United States. For example, the practice of breaking up the family unit, common to the US, was uncommon in most all these other regions. In fact, some of those countries had laws on the books preventing such transactions, and in some rare cases, the enslaved were able to sue slaveholders if they did.

(What If...?)

I'm going to present a loosely based, perhaps factually exaggerated hypothetical scenario to make a point: What if you were having a family barbecue by the river. It included your wife and two children, your parents and sister's nuclear family of four, encompassing three generations. Other groups of people were out enjoying themselves as well when suddenly a group of "Marauders" raced across the bridge with weapons in hand and kidnapped your sister's entire family. Being caught off guard, you were unable to respond before they escaped back across the bride. I ask how would you have responded?

Immediately afterward, others in the area rushed to the remaining family, attempting to console them. Perhaps they said it was a regular occurrence, and they knew where your family was being held. I wonder if they were told their family would be put on ships and taken on a long voyage, bound and chained for some lands unknown thousands of miles away overseas, never to return.

Were they told their family would be forced to work these other peoples' lands, planting seeds and harvesting grains, berries, fruits and vegetables, cotton, and tobacco, and forced to tend their livestock and build their homes, barns, and sheds?

Were they told their meal choices would be limited to everything considered the throw-away parts of the pig from head to toe, including its guts and entrails, served with side dishes of beans, corn, rice, and yams with palm oil and water? By the way, the pig is one of the animal foods designated as "unclean" in the Bible's dietary laws written in The book of Leviticus. Could this be a primary reason the people of my heritage generally suffer from high blood pressure, diabetes, and cholesterol issues today?

Did they know they'd be fashionably dressed and outfitted with the very latest ragtag hand-me-downs, allowing for the flexibility to lift, tote, push, and haul heavy equipment, tools, and materials?

Were they informed their "state of the art" living facilities would consist of shacks they had to build, complete with environmentally uncontrolled air conditioning (during winter) and sweltering heat (during summer) with plumbing (hauled from the nearest well), with sanitation and waste management provided by an outhouse?

Were they told they'd be raped and forced to breed for the purposes of wealth building or forced to manage and maintain other people's households with cooking, cleaning, and caring for the children and adults' smallest details and individual personal needs? Were they told it would have to be done without them ever getting paid? In other words, were they told they would be enslaved?

(The Marauded Becomes The Marauder)

What did the remaining family do at that point? Did they just sit there listening before going back to their grilling as if nothing had happened? The fact was, they soon started helping the abductors! They began gathering others for the taking when the Marauders returned. The "marauded" became the "Marauders."

The "New Abductors" would be rewarded with what amounts to trinkets and some food options other than the meals they provided the abductees. It was said that eventually, the original "Marauders" returned to their original form of stealing people as they had initially, thereby cutting out the middleman and the trading of trinkets or exotic foods. By the way, pig guts are marketed primarily in our communities today as "Chitterlings," pronounced "Chitlins."

You might think the remaining family members would have immediately gathered other family and friends to go after the "Marauders" to retrieve their hijacked family. But that didn't happen! They kicked them/us to the "proverbial" curb, even after learning of the disdainful treatment. You left "us" abandoned, weakened, vulnerable, and all alone. To add insult to injury, today, you treat us with disgust as if you didn't have anything to do with the slave trade.

I don't want to assume, so I ask my "African" cousins, do you feel as if we are less than you, less than pure, or some kind of mutt race? For the most part, you don't seem to want to interact with your cousins here in America. I never see us working in your shops, venues, or places of business, and I'm not alone in feeling you turn your nose up at us.

To be fair, I did play with a band that played at a Senegalese restaurant once a month for 12 plus years. For most of those years, the group of four, sometimes five, had to split a grand total of $120 between us and whatever tips we generated. We played two 45-minute sets. After 10 years of service, the owners increased our overall pay to $140. For most musicians I know, the "MINIMUM" individual pay for a single set is $50. And that's dirt cheap!

The ownership also provided a meal to each performer totaling no more than $15 from the menu. About a year after having a stroke, I stopped playing with the group. I know I'm blessed that God allowed me to primarily rehabilitate myself. However, I was hauling three saxophones, a flute, a music stand, and a portable sound system. It simply became physically exhausting at the time, and personally, I felt we permitted ourselves to be re-enslaved of sorts.

(Get On The Boat For A Ride You'll Never Forget, aka The Middle Passage)

Our now enchained ancestors were packed into the bowels of these ships that only rats tolerated, like the proverbial "Sardines in a can." And when I say bowels on a regular basis, it was literally that. The only times these ships were clean were on their maiden voyage.

To prevent planning for uprisings, with few exceptions, the enchained were pinned down in one location under lock and key in the bottoms of these ships for the entirety of the ocean crossing where they ate, slept, and released their bodily waste and most often died. Being chained as they were set up sores on their wrists and ankles that got infected with gangrene. These unsanitary conditions fostered diseases like dysentery, measles, scurvy, and smallpox. Death, therefore, ran rampant.

Decomposing bodies could lie for days, weeks, or more before being thrown overboard to awaiting sharks that followed these ships for regular meals. I heard it said to this very day sharks still travel these old routes. On rare occasions, they were brought above deck for a rinse-off. Women and children were occasionally given a little more leeway to move about the ship, but they all were basically in the same predicament.

This leg of the trade became known as "The Middle Passage." Voyages initially lasted around 6 months, but as crews became more efficient, the time was reduced to about six weeks. When it came to providing meals, the enchained normally would be fed once a day, if at all, of the same "sumptuous" foods they would be fed during their future enslavement.

If supplies ran low, which was often, the crew was given first priority. These unsavory crewmen, who could only get work on these ships due to having seedy criminal backgrounds, were primarily responsible for transmitting syphilis and other diseases. On these ships, they were free to exercise their demons and engage their most devious and perverted desires and proclivities, where they regularly raped the women and girls and, sometimes, the men and boys. I once heard a story that purported an entire family was raped in such a manner. As gross or exaggerated as it might sound, I'm sure it's based on truth and did happen, likely more than once.

Now, place yourself in the scenario I described earlier of a sister's entire family being abducted. Imagine, as a man, father, and husband, you hear your wife getting brutally raped by crewmen! Another night, you heard your young virgin daughter getting gang raped! A week later, it was your teenage son being anally brutalized, and the next week, your family heard you getting anally assaulted. Can you begin to imagine how powerless you would have felt and the level of humiliation and trauma you and your family would have suffered and endured? And, it often was a recurring event! You would likely have become depressed, fearful, helpless, and hopeless.

All this disease and depression resulted in very high mortality rates amongst the enchained. Only 5% of the roughly 12.5 million brought to these shores survived the Middle Passage voyage. This meant roughly 250 million or a quarter of a billion lives were lost in the transport to the United States alone. This doesn't account for the rest of the Americas and the Caribbean Sea.

Talk about a holocaust! As of the 2020 census, the United States population is 329.5 million. 250 million is approaching our current national population today, which is more than many countries in the modern world. What a horrific and tragic loss of life! Was anybody screaming, "All Lives Matter," then? Let alone "Black Lives Matter."

Uncounted death tolls occurred because many enchained individuals became depressed due to their loss of freedoms, family, and the lack of general civility and humanity and refused to eat. This led to forced feedings. Others committed suicide when brought up to the deck by jumping overboard, leading to the installation of nets around the ship's perimeter to reduce their loss of "potential profit."

Other measures taken to discourage suicide and rebellion included crewmen beating enchained individuals, often to the point of death, then sometimes cutting out the hearts and livers and feeding them to the other enchained people who were forced to watch. Slaves were considered expensive, high-priced commodities and investments, generally costing $800-$1,200. Today that would translate to $32,000-$48,000.

(After 400 Years, Traitor Ancestors, What Did You Get Out Of It All?)

I've heard some people say…

"Why should I care about you."

"If you don't care about yourself?"

And I added:

And when you are treacherous unto thyself.

So, what did our "Trader Ancestors" get for haggling and selling off their children, and what does it mean today for all the people around the world sharing my ancestry? Googling the subject, you can learn a wealth of information on how extensive the involvement of not only the European and Akebulan (African) countries but, shockingly, how the Native Indigenous people traded with Europeans and how it also partially led to their demise because of the devastating diseases they caught resulting from these interactions and sometimes on purpose like the "polio blankets." However, my primary focus is the relationship and interaction of my ancestors from the mother continent as they traded their own people with the Europeans for what amounts to trinkets and things of little to no value.

In return for selling off our ancestors, our Continental ancestors routinely received manufactured products of clothing from India and Europe that included shirts, jackets, cloaks, gowns, belts and threads. Unworked or semi-processed metals: Iron bars, Copper rods, Lead, occasional Gold and Silver. Metal wares: Basins, pots & pans, and knives. Firearms: Gunpowder, beads, coral, and cowries. Alcohol: Rum, Gin, Beer, and wine; tobacco, glassware, and exotic foods. Various coastal rulers received pompous gifts or status symbols consisting of Satin robes, brocaded silk and gold trimmed French hats, music boxes, Silverware and more. It was an uneven trade for human lives.

Is there ever a fair trade for human life? I heard a saying somewhere that essentially goes, "Why should I treat you right when you don't treat yourself right?" I would also add, "And when you treat yourselves treacherously." Since the Atlantic slave trade, Western and Central Alkebulan went bankrupt because the slave trade also extended well into the interior of the continent (Marauded becoming Marauders).

In fact, worldwide, all the children of Akebulan heritage have suffered financially and politically. Generally, the entire Continent was affected and devastated. The land was literally stolen from under the feet of the native population, where huge swaths of lands and territories were apportioned by European countries, namely Britain, France, Germany, Belgium, Portugal, Spain, and Italy, still affecting the continent today.

These colonies quickly commenced to striping, ripping, and raping the land of its resources, with all the profits and riches going to them, their posterity, and countries. The amassed wealth they've accumulated for themselves left Alkebulan bankrupt, backward thinking, diseased and desperately despondent, and in a state of confusion and hopelessness, devoid of decency, growth, or integrity, which continues to this very day with a few exceptions.

And because the continent still possess rare raw materials that are essential to the operations of today's computer industry, artificial intelligence, and green technologies, countries like China have positioned themselves to continue the rip-off. They also import Chinese laborers. This denies the native populations jobs and opportunities to accumulate wealth. Hello, Rodney Dangerfield.

It appears to me that since the period of the Atlantic slave trade, the world seems to have given the middle finger to the people who share my heritage here in America, back on the Alkebulan continent, and all around the world in general. Simply look at what's happened to the continent since "You," our trader ancestors, first bartered off, then neglected us, your own family.

These highly valued raw and rare materials, essential to technologies past and present, have rarely benefitted the people native to the area. Although there are some exceptions, just look at how desecrated, diseased, and destitute many of people are in general, spanning the entire continent. As history has documented and we continue to observe, all the people of Akebulan heritage have suffered. The troubling part is our continental ancestors weren't programmed by the "Willie Lynch" letter. More about him and his letter later.

Again, if someone from who-knows-where came onto your property, then started digging around in your backyard and found all kinds of rare elements, gemstones, and precious metals, then claimed them all for themselves and, by the way, left your backyard torn up, how would you feel about it? So I ask our "Trader Ancestors," was it a fair trade for selling human life and that of the best of your children? From my perspective, I would emphatically answer, HELL NAWL!

(From Sugar To Shit)

"To the victor goes the spoils" is *a commonly misquoted saying that actually goes, "To the victory belong the Spoils of the enemy."*

By William L. Marcy

As stated previously, this quote insinuates the winners of great battles and wars get to call the shots and change the rules as they see fit. Also, we know history has been "Hellenized," with the (MDW-NTR) "Medur-Neter" or "Medur-Netchur" being called "Hieroglyphics." The writing system developed in Kemet didn't make use of vowels. However, since the slave trade, Akebulan has been treated like the "Rodney Dangerfield" of continents. It gets "No Respect."

Antarctica is treated better. And again, all the children born from the continent worldwide have been victimized since you, our "Trader Ancestors," kicked us to the curb. It's unavoidable when some members of a family are mistreated, the entire family suffers in some way or form or fashion. Prior to tearing apart the fabric of the people on the continent, our ancestors shared ideal conditions and circumstances that were perfect for them to thrive and become great. And they did!

According to documented modern-day scientific technology explaining DNA, the first Homo Sapiens-Sapiens humans sprung up from the Sub-Saharan region of Alkebulan, which translates to "Mother of Mankind" or the "Garden of Eden." In actuality, it was the bones of the woman anthropologist named "Lucy" (or "Degnesh" by the native population) found in Ethiopia. We call it Sub-Saharan today but according to historical climate studies, it was the time before the region was a desert.

Before its current boundaries were re-set at the Berlin Conference of 1884-85, the original Akebulan continent extended further east into the ancient Mesopotamian region through to the Indian Ocean. While populating the entire Alkebulan continent, humans inevitably traveled further north around the Mediterranean Sea and west into Europe. Then east and north into Turkey and Russia and further east and southeast into Asia and China.

From northern Russia, they traveled across the then-land bridge of the Bering Straits into North America, then Southward all the way down to the tip of South America, and finally into Antarctica before it became the frozen continent it is today. At the current rate of global warming/climate change, we are likely to see that culture will reveal itself there as well. I've seen some very old (Piri Reis) maps that suggest such. They also traveled south in boats to Australia and the Polynesian Islands. There's evidence they traveled in ships using the coastal currents west across the Atlantic Ocean into the Americas.

Simultaneously, our earlier ancestors continued cultivating and developing their thinking processes while seeding cultures and civilizations and devising writing systems and later institutions of "Higher Learning," like, for example, the one considered to be the world's first and oldest continuously operating University in Timbuktu, Mali since the 1100s aka the Sankore Mosque and University, established by King Mansa Musa, who is said to be the world's richest man of all time. Homo Sapiens, aka "Mankind," also developed sophisticated Astronomy, Science and Mathematics.

And because the entire Alkebulan continent is in a temperate zone, our ancestors began experimenting with farming techniques and learning how to cultivate wide varieties of seeds, grains, nuts, fruits, and vegetables. They forged kingdoms and empires while building the unrivaled, unparalleled, and, as of today, the never duplicated structures called "Pyramids" all along the way and all around the world. The Pyramids are the only remaining visual structural evidence of the ancient world known as one of the "7 wonders of the world." Homo Sapiens mankind multiplied and dispersed civilization all across the globe and into the most remote locations.

Thousands of years later, some dispersed civilizations like the Greeks and Romans, aka "the great copiers," seeking the highest of knowledge, returned back to the native continent. To this very day, so much of what is considered "our style," which includes our general mannerism and language idiosyncrasies, are initially condemned, then condoned, later copied and commercialized, then consumed worldwide. Today, for example, special emphasis can be placed on our musical art forms. An example of this historical copying would be the doctors of the world recitation of the "Hippocratic Oath."

It was Imhotep (Hellenized as Asclepius), the "original man of science" and actual "Father of Medicine," who was known to have performed surgeries that are only now being realized by modern medicine. Amongst them are Open Heart Surgery, Caesarean Sections, and Brain Surgery, as well as a variety of dental procedures, and he was know for being the first to heal with plant-based herbal medicinal remedies(8). His knowledge was also lost and likely burned in Alexandria. Perhaps this is why, over the centuries, history is replete with brutal and savage attempts at surgeries that have only begun to seem humane in the 20th century.

Maybe this is also the reason the medical profession is still today called a "practice," with all of humanity being its guinea pig. His genius also extended into Architecture. It was Imhotep who planned and built the first Pyramid structures(9). The Greeks carried "only some" of his knowledge of medical procedures back to Greece and failed to pay him proper historical homage or give him his due credit. Eventually, they falsely claimed his knowledge as their own. This exaltation of the "Hippocratic Oath" came (only) after the Greeks and Romans reneged on their original teachers and began invading their lands and conquering its people. With the Hellenization of Imhotep to Asclepius, "To the victory goes the spoils,"... And history is rewritten.

(Baby Mama Drama)

One troublesome issue manifesting itself in our community has been the inconsistency of the father's presence in the household. During the enslavement period, this absence was often by design as a result of the slaveholders purposefully splitting up families. Sometimes done for financial reasons, the end result was a weakened structural family unit. Obviously, an immeasurable amount of heartbreak and stress was placed on a family by splitting them up regardless of who was removed. Can you begin to empathize and understand the indescribable daily emotional trauma a parent, especially a mother, experienced for the rest of her life, worrying about the condition and state of being of her child?

Today, the term for that condition is known as "Toxic Stress," made known to the public via the broadcast news media as a result of the practices former president $kunk enacted at the Southern border with Mexico. He permitted border patrol to rip children away from their parents (primarily their mothers) as they sought refuge and citizenship here in America in their attempt to escape the horrors in their Central and South American countries. Studies have shown that "Toxic Stress" affects you to your very core, going so deeply that it alters your DNA!

After the enslavement era and from the Reconstruction period onward, other measures were taken to deprive our fathers of our families, including lynching, extended imprisonment for petty Acts (aka the Black Codes), and the enactment of legislated laws and certain other economic measures (last hired, first fired) designed to deprive fathers of a means of supporting their families. Of course, this placed intense psychological stress on his psyche as it relates to the historical and traditional role of the father with regard to his self-esteem and his manhood (RSWS: 1, 2, & 6).

Later, laws were also enacted denying mothers financial assistance for their children if the father was also living in the household (RSWS: 5). It was called the "Welfare" program. Today there's an unwritten law but clearly observable rule that has come into practice. This is to hire more of the women of our heritage rather than the men. This is fundamental to the Willie Lynch letter, which pits males against females. This practice often results in our women ignorantly looking down in condemnation on our men for their inability to acquire gainful employment (RSWS: 1, 4, & 8).

Since we've been programmed to go against each other, sometimes we might act against our own self-interest and what's best for our families. One such syndrome is known in our community as "Baby Mama Drama." From my observations, Baby Mama Drama occurs most often when a child is born out of wedlock then the mother denies the father/child relationship by withholding the child from the father in an attempt to manipulate or punish him as a result of her disgust or anger towards him for whatever reason(s).

This seems to happen most often when the father has a level of education, is working, shows interest in being actively involved in the child's life, and has the means and desire to support the child. It happened more frequently before the emergence of Father's Rights attorneys. On the opposite end of the spectrum, the way I've seen it, this didn't happen nearly as frequently to the so-called "deadbeat dad."

Although each situation is unique and varies in circumstances, often the situation reverses when the "deadbeat dad," who may not have gone to college, possibly with limited or low-paying employment, perhaps involves being previously incarcerated, addicted, and/or is a "womanizer." At any rate, he most often demonstrated little to no ability or interest in spending quality time or providing any physical, emotional, or monetary support for the child.

He might've even outright denied and/or objected to the child being his. In many of these circumstances, I've observed the mother trying to "push" the child off on the "so-called" father as often as possible. However, both scenarios usually profoundly influence and affect the child/father relationship, especially the child.

The following story is a true case of "Baby Mama Drama" that I personally was able to observe. It will be a little lengthy because it happened to a close friend of mine. In this account, all the names have been changed to protect the innocent and because it is personal and private information.

(Parallel Universe)

After graduating from College, like most musicians, I needed a job. That following August, I learned from my future sister-in-law about a part-time position in the mailroom at the University where she worked. I applied and got the job. A couple months later, another young man of my heritage, Bobby Walton, was also hired part-time. We quickly became friends and got to know each other. We found we shared several things in common, like being born months apart in Cook County Hospital, with Bobby growing up on the west-side and me on the south-side.

We both graduated College with bachelor's Degrees in Music Performance from HBCUs in North Carolina, with my degree on flute (sax) and his on keyboards. We learned that our College football teams and bands had competed against each other a couple times. However, due to scheduling, the bands rarely got an opportunity to interact and mingle with each other. Our friendship quickly developed and bonded by hanging out together during lunch breaks and after work. Roughly 2 years later, we were both hired full-time, again a couple months apart.

Upon our hiring, there were two other older men sharing our heritage. James Matteson, who held Computer Science and Political Science degrees from the University, who was about 10 years older than us and Jeff Billings, who held an Associate's Degree. Jeff was also the former top guy for the

Mailing Services department and was just barely old enough to be our father. Before Bobby was hired, James learned I was a musician and introduced me to his cousin, Zack, a prolific composer and keyboard player.

After a couple weeks of working with him, Zack introduced me to the band he was performing with, and they took me into the fold. About a month later, a local franchise restaurant owner approached us with the idea of producing a record. Things moved very quickly. The group's leadership signed the deal and we recorded in November, about a month after I had met Bobby. I got him into the group just after we completed the album, which first aired on WCGI and WBMX radio in Chicago during the week between Christmas and New Year's, leading into 1984.

A high school bandmate had visited me and I shared the recording with him. When he left, he returned within a minute, saying it was playing on the radio. The DJ was introducing our record for the first time, and I turned on the radio as they dropped the needle on the first beat. It was a thrill like no other to hear it for the first time on the radio as chills ran through my body.

In a twist of irony, Bobby, who didn't record a track, got credit on every track as one of the keyboard players, and my credits got screwed up on my flute, saxophone, and vocal work. That had no effect on our budding friendship. In fact, it grew closer and tighter as we played and partied together, becoming each other's "wingman." A couple years after being hired full-time, we learned the University offered two free classes per semester to full-time employees. We had been told music classes were the only exception to the policy. A couple years later, we learned music courses were offered only if you were majoring and seeking to earn an Education degree or certification.

After learning the requirements to earn our Illinois Teacher's Certification, Bobby and I decided to share an apartment to consolidate our resources. The final requirement demanded we perform a 16-week period of student teaching, meaning both of us would have to take a 4-months leave of absence from the same job and space at the same time. Our jobs could be jeopardized, but at least over the 4 years of part-time school, we had saved up for the event.

To his credit, our supervisor, who was also a musician, cleared us both to student teach and return. Another parallel in our lives was, after a couple years of full time employment, we both met our girlfriends at the University around the same time while delivering mail. Both of them were receptionists. As a result of sharing an apartment, our lady friends became friends, too. They both got pregnant around the same time. My woman got pregnant about 2 months before Bobby's, but as fate would have it, our daughters were born about 2 weeks apart because Bobby's woman had some complications during her pregnancy and prematurely gave birth at 7 months.

(Convergence of Divergence)

Here's where our lives began to diverge. During the pregnancies, Bobby's enthusiasm infected me too. He wanted to name his child, which motivated me to do the same. We researched and selected boy and girl names that were meaningful. My women agreed with the names I picked out, and so did Bobby's initially. But unbeknownst to him, she reneged upon her birth and gave their daughter her last name. His daughter's original name was beautiful to me and would have meant, "The resurrection" is "peaceful and serene" and "gift(s) of God." When she reneged, her last name changed from "gift(s) of God" to "the dweller from the meadow from residence nearby."

So Bobby began searching for their apartment, thinking his women had agreed to his name choices. They began discussing plans to get married, which again made me briefly consider it. My woman had her own apartment, and Bobby's partner still lived in her family's house. I was thrilled when my daughter was born! However, a couple weeks later, due to the premature birth of his baby, Bobby was immediately stressed. There was the uncertainty of life for his child and he hadn't secured their apartment.

Now, like brothers, I felt his pain, fears, stress, and anxiety. Recalling him getting the call at work, he rushed to the hospital, knowing his baby was 2 months early. After work, I hurried to the hospital to give him moral support but was only able to speak with him briefly. When he described what he saw, it left me feeling that might be the only time he would see his baby girl.

Obviously, I wasn't permitted to see mother and child, but what disturbed me most was his description of the baby having no chest cavity. She had shoulders and a stomach, but in between was a depression that he said resembled a pothole and that she was struggling for every breath. I went to the bathroom to collect my emotions. He had two priorities at that point, being at the hospital every day supporting his "fiancé" and newborn and finding an apartment for them to come home to.

I felt his daughter was quite strong to have overcome that first day alone. He told me her birth weight was 3 lbs 5 oz. She initially lost a couple "crucial ounces" before being stabilized and started gaining weight. He told me the most critical issue before she could leave the hospital was to develop the ability to suck or drink from the bottle. However, the baby's mother was also having difficulty producing milk. Bobby was convinced the first milk should be mother's milk. He shared how difficult it was for her to produce enough breast milk for the baby's first suckling. He was there every day, supporting them and encouraging her to produce the milk. He informed me that they had literally squeezed enough breast milk from her and stuck the tiny bottle of milk into the baby's mouth, and she immediately began to suck and gain weight.

I learned that some mammals, including women, can have problems producing milk. Nature demonstrates when some mammals have problems producing milk others of their species often play a surrogate role. I heard it happened with humans in the past centuries. I don't know how that would have played out at the time or today for that matter because [breast] feeding is a part of the natural bonding process between mother and child.

I do understand some of the reasons many women choose not to breastfeed. However, I wonder whether the world would've experienced a formula milk shortage, as I heard happened during the COVID-19 pandemic. God created all mammals with the ability to produce milk naturally. Studies reveal that mother's milk is obviously the most nourishing and fortifying substance for the babies' intestines and immune systems. However, don't accuse me of being the Supreme Court and trying to tell a woman what to do with her body.

After a couple weeks, I finally got a chance to see the baby. She was so tiny. Bobby told me when he held her for the first time, she could fit in the palm of his hand, extending from his middle finger to his wrist. When I saw her, she was restrained inside an incubator with needles sticking out of her forehead and arms due to jaundice. From what I learned, premature babies normally stay in the hospital for the balance of the normal pregnancy. Bobby's baby only spent a little more than a month because after getting that milk, she progressed rapidly and gained the necessary required minimum weight of 4 pounds to leave early.

Bobby got the apartment just in time to receive them. He felt so proud and, like me, doted over his daughter. It was one of the happiest times of both our lives because I felt exactly as he did. It was something about becoming a parent that made me feel responsible and deeply committed to something other than myself. I felt protective and wanted to shield her from any hurt or harm. Before that, I loved my mother more than anyone, but the birth of my daughter was deeper and more profound than anything else I ever felt. I can't fully explain it, and I'm sure all loving parents understand exactly what I mean.

Bobby's experience illustrates the "baby mama drama" I observe plaguing our communities in the way I'm speaking. We still hadn't yet completed our student teaching requirement when Bobby moved out to form his new family unit. Being best friends, we knew everything that was going on in each other's lives, but here's where the problems in his life began manifesting. Because of some complications resulting from the premature birth, his "fiancé" didn't return to work for about 2 years.

So Bobby was holding down all the financial responsibilities, but according to him, she was receiving some sort of assistance and agreed to handle the electric and cooking gas bills. He told me she had to pay only about $5 a month for cooking gas because they had radiators for heat. The electric bill wasn't that much either for their one bedroom apartment. He handled the rent, food, phone, and everything else.

Several months into their cohabitation, he started telling me how lazy she was. She came from a family of females consisting of her mother, an aunt, and three older sisters. He said he figured she had shared household chores as he was raised to do. Whatever the case, she didn't do anything around the apartment except cook occasionally. They lived in a building that housed a Laundromat, yet unclean clothes lay all over the apartment. The same for unwashed dishes and the apartment was always dusty and smelled of diapers. He felt it became generally unsanitary and that he was doing everything including cleaning up after her after coming home from work. He was becoming increasingly frustrated.

Once he told me that after she ate some ice cream, she sat the bowl down on the floor. This time, he didn't pick it up because he wanted to see how long it would take for her to put it in the sink. 2 weeks later, the bowl was still in the same place now with sticky dust in it. On top of all that, she was putting on the pounds in an unattractive way. He was blowing off steam with me, and I advised him to talk to her about how he felt. Weeks later, he told me he had an uncomfortable conversation, but nothing seemed to change. He got the apartment with the intent to marry her but was beginning to seriously doubt if it was the wisest move to make. He loved his daughter and wanted to be there for her. He was motivated by the fact he had never known his own father.

They had been living together for more than a year when he told me he couldn't understand why she began to argue and "snap" at him for no reason. He thought maybe it was because he'd asked her to contribute more around the apartment. It was about 16 months or so into their cohabitation when he came to work, so upset he was shaking. He told me he felt she didn't love him anymore because she was arguing all the time.

On this particular day before coming to work, she struck him in the face with keys in her hand that hit him in the eye. Like me, he was raised with the understanding that you don't hit women. That was something that came up in our conversation years ago when I shared with him the philosophy my mother imparted to her sons. She said, "You never hit a woman…unless she hits you first." He said when the keys hit him in his eyes, upon reflex, he slapped her once. He shared how bad he felt about it all and was quiet all day.

The next day, when he came to work, he had tears in his eyes. He revealed he asked her to go back to her mother's house to live. I knew it was one of the hardest things he ever had to do, particularly because of how much he loved his daughter. She was the highlight and center of his life. I really felt for him. It turned out she had not kept up her end of the financial agreement either, which left him in debt because all the bills were in his name.

(Only The Beginning Of His Troubles)

Out of respect for my friend confiding in me, I will summarize his plight from this point as he dealt with his "baby mama drama." After the breakup and her move back to her family's house, he moved back in with me but had to sleep on the couch because he tossed out his twin-sized bed for her queen-sized brass bed. Oddly, it was difficult for him to establish credit. I was with him when he literally had to beg a furniture store to grant him credit to buy a bed.

Since we still hadn't completed our student teaching requirement, on days we didn't have class, Bob visited his daughter. He continued on almost a daily basis for years, even after being hired by CPS. He'd spend an hour or 2 per visit singing to, playing with, and reading to his daughter and in conversation with the baby's grandmother.

The issue then became his inability to take his daughter anywhere with him. He told me it felt as if he were under some kind of supervised visitation, and over the years, he became increasingly frustrated that he couldn't take her to visit family on his side, not even for Father's Day. He said that he went along with the program to keep peace and stability for Baby Girl as she began to grow up. Eventually, baby mama got her own apartment near her mother's house, and he started visiting her there, that's if the baby mama didn't pretend "not" to be home. Often, Baby Girl still went to Grandma's house after school.

Bobby continued making requests to take her for visits on weekends and holidays so she could get to know all her family, with the now usual negative results. She started telling him, "We'll talk!" After several years of teaching,

Bobby decided to buy a house in the same neighborhood as Grandma and Baby Mama. He had set aside a bedroom for her with all the trimmings. Then, one day, as it was approaching Father's Day, it all came to a head. He told me he saw baby mama in the nearby McDonalds.

While getting coffee, he asked her again if he could pick her up on Father's Day but got the usual refusal and the now customary "we'll talk" line. For the next couple of days, he was unable to see his young one because Mama didn't answer the bell. So he went to Grandma's house as usual but Baby Girl wasn't there either, although on one of those days, he said he was certain he saw baby mama's curtains move.

On his next day's visit, "Baby Mama" had a male visitor for the first time. He felt that was her business and did his usual thing with his daughter. As the visit concluded, he again requested to pick up Baby Girl for Father's Day, but this time, she seemed to get indignant.

As the story goes, she sent Baby Girl to her room, opened her front door, then pointed to it, rolled her neck, and shouted, "I said we'll talk. Now get out!" He told me he felt as if it was protest time! Felt like he was at a 1960s sit-in at a Southern lunch counter because she had company and was "showing out." He replied, "I'm tired of all this we'll talk stuff. I want a yes or no right now!" She became livid, then started screaming and literally jumping up and down, saying she was going to call the police. He said he'd never seen her act that way, and as he sat there, he calmly said, "So."

Then she picked up that old heavy landline phone receiver as if to call the police and began striking him on top of his head and in his face. She had gotten in several blows before he could react and stand up to shield himself. Angered, he said his mind simultaneously went to two places. Never hit a girl unless she hits you first and to Muhammad Ali. As he stood up in defense while she was still hitting him, he said he ducked and weaved, then slugged her once in the face. He later learned she'd gotten a black eye. She then kicked him on his buttocks, and he said he reciprocated then ran out the already opened door into the Hallway where some additional words were exchanged like, "Do you really want some of this?"

He reflected on how he never felt so angry or embarrassed and exhilarated all at the same time and noted that her visitor sat there the entire time without a peep! As he vented, he said he thought maybe the guy noticed how petty and violent she was acting because a dad was trying to spend time with his daughter on Father's Day. I'm sure he vented with some family members, too.

He decided they needed some distance, reasoning she was trying to provoke him into violence because her sister was an attorney with the District Attorney's office in Chicago. He didn't want to get an arrest record, feeling it could affect his ability to teach and his livelihood. Like me, he was a peace-loving, mild-mannered guy who hadn't shown any violent tendencies in all the time I knew him. It was emotionally painful because it stopped him from spending any time with his daughter.

He started thinking about what he could do in the meantime. I reminded him that I had set up an annuity and bank account several years ago for my daughter in addition to child support payments. He set up the bank account but had difficulty with the annuity. Later that year, Bob received a summons to go to court for child support. It seemed baby mama was also seeking retroactive support as well. To his fortune, he'd established her bank account and had made hefty contributions to it. Bob argued he attempted to set up an annuity and tried getting her on his medical plan and that he had supported them both for nearly 2 years in their apartment. As a result, the judge determined he didn't have to pay retroactive support but stated he could now legally set up the annuity and get her medical coverage. As with me, he paid child support until she graduated college.

Through the years, he shared his plight with other family and friends and basically got similar responses from almost all of them, which was, "Don't worry, as she gets older, she'll understand and seek to have a relationship with you. Your actions have already demonstrated that you love her." Privately, he expressed to me that he didn't feel confident about that becoming a reality. I clearly saw he was still disparaged, depressed, and heartbroken. The issue of a father's rights and obtaining an attorney hadn't come to the forefront as it has in recent years.

(Hope Springs Eternal...?)

After he started paying child support, both his previously denied requests for the annuity and health insurance coverage were granted. The health insurance was most important because she wasn't being covered under her mother's job. His actions later turned out to be a blessing in disguise. It must have been when our daughters entered 6th grade that Bobby's Baby Mama decided to start attending his church. He said it was awkward at first because several church members knew of his experiences with her. However, he always sat with them during services. He also felt she was trying to reconcile in some way.

I suggested he give his daughter private lessons on an instrument, as I had begun with my daughter over the summer. He brought it up to mother and daughter, and they agreed. He started picking her up from Grandma's for lessons at his house a couple times a week, and her mother would pick her up from there. About a year later, Bob shared something deeply personal and private.

Baby Mama revealed to him why she was arguing and snapping and struck him back then, which led to their parting of ways. She got pregnant again while they were living together but lost the baby! He said knowing that would've made all the difference. He could've been more supportive and understanding because he was in love. I personally felt it wasn't fair to him because, after all, it was his unborn child, too. The stereotype has been that men don't communicate.

Sometime after that, Baby Mama decided to join the church's choir, of which Bob was the choir director. It also seemed many in his congregation were encouraging them to get married. He told me in the spirit of Christ, he had forgiven her but still had to be true to himself. He simply didn't feel that passionate love he once felt for her. Friendship was the best he could do at that point because too much damage had been done over too long a period. He also felt he was finally developing that real father/daughter relationship he always desired.

Both our daughters gained membership to the same City performing group in the 7th grade, which allowed our families to finally meet each other. After his daughter entered her freshmen year, for some reason, she stopped playing. Of course, I asked him why. He told me she said she didn't want any other music teacher to teach her besides him. It sounded weak to me, but I can't judge that?

Ironically, after her freshmen year, the band director's position became available at her school. Bob applied for the job and got it. He was thrilled, and I was happy for him/them too. He figured this would get her playing again and give him an automatic helper to assist with his program, as well as put him in the position to help her and other students earn scholarships as he had. He could also take her to and from school. Perfect! Things were looking up until…

When he shared the good news with his daughter, she told him she didn't want to ride back and forth to school with him or join the band and didn't want anybody to know that he was her father! Awkward, because he knew a couple of her elementary school classmates who also went to her High School! They had attended a "Classical" school where there was only one class per grade level, and the entire class remained together throughout their elementary school years, which was up through 6th grade.

They then tested to qualify to attend certain selected high schools that kept them together with a designed curriculum to transition them into their regular high school after their freshmen year. With that, he knew the damage had been done, and what he feared most had been realized. He would never have the daddy/daughter relationship he always sought.

He was utterly devastated and felt it was the worst year of his life in several ways. She never once visited him in the band room. He told me he only saw her two or three times by chance in the halls. He changed schools after that year because of her abandonment. The other reasons I won't discuss. I felt really bad for him. That was cold-blooded! I had witnessed his unending sacrifices of love for her. He didn't get to take prom pictures because she didn't let him know when the actual event occurred, although he asked her about it. And yes, he could've contacted the school but that didn't guarantee certain particular details.

Most fathers would want to know who escorted his daughter to the prom, the dress she was wearing and all the traditional pomp and circumstance surrounding the event. I knew he was looking forward to doing his part. He learned after the fact that she and her Elementary School girlfriends went together in a limousine. Bob and his mother did attend her High School graduation and only got to briefly see her after the ceremony before she was whisked away by baby mama's family for dinner, etc....

He was shocked that she chose to leave the city to go to college because of how her mother tried to keep her under her wing. I guess she had a similar sense of adventure as he did. When it came to her College graduation, it was no better. Although he helped finance her education at perhaps the most well-known and prestigious HBCU, she never once contacted him until graduation when he and his mother traveled to Maryland only to be able to spend about a half hour with her before she again was whisked away by baby mama's family.

He told me that his mother, who was one of the people always encouraging him that their relationship would eventually work out, was deeply hurt by the entire affair, especially because her own granddaughter didn't invite them to have dinner with her mother's side. His mother was stoic at the time and only revealed it to him several years later. He told me he was so used to being mistreated that it didn't faze him at the time. He was just pleasantly surprised he'd gotten an invitation to the graduation at all. It was only after his mother shared her feelings about the event that his heart ached for her disappointed feelings.

Like most students not on scholarship, his daughter accumulated "Student Debt." And after she got a job, Bob felt it was time to turn the annuity over to her to handle with some advice on using it to assist in paying down her debt while still allowing it to grow. She likely had enough to pay off her entire debt because my daughter was in a similar position because she had just graduated college with an annuity also. However, my daughter did earn a partial band scholarship, which offset some of her expenses and I had started my daughter's annuity a couple years earlier than he had. I turned my daughter's annuity over to her after she got a job as well. We knew at age 21 they technically controlled them anyway, and we were just paying at that point. He told me he felt she had likely changed her beneficiary to her mother anyway.

(Always There)

After her graduation, we saw her once over the summer. I say we because Bobby and I were invited to some eclectic art show that also featured nude female models painted in body art. As fate would have it, we ran into none other than his "baby girl." I hadn't seen her since the last City Concert, where both our daughters participated when they were in 8th grade. Bobby was trying hard to contain himself but I could see how proud of her he was. She was a beautiful young lady now and a pretty version of him. As I've heard said in my community, he spit her out!

The following September, Bobby told me she had to have a biopsy performed on her birthday for possible blood cancer. Wow! This was another devastating and surprising turn of events. The biopsy came up positive, and she entered the hospital in October. There he was again, just like when she was born, at the hospital every day. A couple weeks later, he shouted out to me, "Thank God for Obamacare!" Then showed me the bill for her first 2 weeks of hospital care. It was over $31,000. And it was covered by "Obamacare," aka the "ACA" age extension to his health plan.

He felt so blessed and grateful she was still able to continue on his health care plan until age 26. He later told me he didn't look at another hospital bill from that point on. She was hospitalized at least a couple months with follow-up chemotherapy treatments. Some people (Repunkicans) in opposition to the enactment of the ACA tried to frighten people with talk of "death panels." The way I saw it, "Obamacare" was life-saving and life-preserving.

From that point forward, whenever we engaged in conversation or activities, I always asked him how was "baby girl" doing. After 5 years in remission, a person is considered cancer-free. It was only a few years later that the cancer came back on his daughter with a vengeance. This time, her medical care spanned several months that included 4-day hospital stays every few weeks, with the culminating event being a two-week stay and stem cell transplant. I visited her on one occasion with Bobby. He confided after the stem cell transplant, he again thought she was going to die, just as when he saw her for the very first time, telling me she was in so much pain that they permitted her to self-medicate with some type of opioid after the transplant. He said the way her eyes were rolling around in her head, he thought she would overdose. Fortunately, she was still being covered by his health plan by the Obamacare extension.

(Finally)

As I said earlier, Bobby's daughter had to be one of the strongest people I was aware of. She got the stem cell transplant and pulled through. Some people don't believe in receiving blood transfusions for religious reasons. I've heard it said that it changes your character, and you begin to take on the personality(s) of others. You've likely heard the sayings "things run in three's" and "the third time is the charm." Well, nearly 5 years passed, and again, here was Bobby telling me his daughter's cancer had come back on her. This time, they introduced some new experimental treatment that encouraged herbal supplements. I'm not exactly sure how long it's been since her last bout with cancer, but so far, so good, and she did ring the 5-year "in remission" bell and seems to be stable, happily working, and travels a bit.

Through all the ups and mostly downs, as with any parent and from what I've observed, Bobby's love for his "baby girl" never waned. I had always included them in my prayers, hoping Bobby would have that close, loving relationship he'd always desired. However, it seems he could never do or say the right things to her. I don't know all the details, but from what he told me, a conversation went along the lines of him saying, "You don't really know me, and I don't really know you. We don't really know each other. In many ways, we're still strangers!"

He told me he didn't feel she understood where he was coming from. We all know how you get to know someone. As with any relationship, it's by spending time with and talking to each other. He was trying to convey that to his daughter when he told me she said, "Well, we can agree to be strangers then." He said, his heart sunk into his stomach.

He was devastated once again, saying she seemed to want to limit their communications to basically birthdays and Father's Day wishes, and over these last several years, that was the extent of her communications via text message. He, by contrast still trying to respect her wishes, would text her anything he deemed to be important or vital information. As the COVID-19 virus struck the world, Bobby contracted the virus, and because we weren't permitted to visit patients during that time, he died alone in the hospital during the summer of 2020. I lost my best friend, and Bobby lost the chance to ever reconcile his relationship with his "baby girl."

(Let Us Hurt Ourselves)

Another issue confronting our community is criminal activity. It's common everywhere around the world. That's why laws, judicial systems, and policing exist in every country, city, and community. Needless to say, some communities are more plagued by crime than others. Normally, the more affluent communities having money matriculating within them usually experience the least amount of criminal issues. Again, I must point out that our communities historically have been purposefully and systematically shut out from community development projects, various financial opportunities, and the prosperity afforded most other communities around the country (RSWS: 1, 2, 4, 5, & 6). Hence, many of our neighborhoods experience higher rates of criminal activity.

Nevertheless, we're not forced to steal from, squabble with, hurt, injure, or kill those within our neighborhoods. What's particularly disturbing to me is the number of self-inflicted senseless shootings and murders. It seems crime is more prevalent today than in my childhood or during the legally segregated era when everyone seemed to know everybody else. Perhaps today's problems are compounded by the influx of illegal drugs, the pent-up tensions of financial stress, and the strife and frustrations that have collectively accumulated within us that we've been unable to release otherwise and then unleash it on each other. Whatever excuses we claim, it still makes no logical or productive sense!

Theft is a troubling issue plaguing neighborhoods. For example, a scandalous neighbor might watch the comings and goings of other neighbors with the intent to break in and steal from them when they leave their residence. They might observe a neighbor bring in a new audio/visual entertainment system then monitor their work and weekend schedule and routines for a period of time before waiting for the "perfect time" to break in and steal that system and/or other items as well.

When I look at the "crack epidemic," the people of my heritage generally haven't had the means of bringing cocaine or any other drugs in mass into the country or our communities, for which it was subsequently dumped. However, upon its arrival, yes we are guilty of selling it to each other. Once a "crackhead" is addicted, they are subject to begging and borrowing or petty thief and prostitution, to more serious vices like armed robbery to support and supply their addiction. Often, it's done within our own community. Many drug dealers are now "claiming turf," or small areas within the neighborhood, and a willing to commit violent acts to protect said turf and even kill for it.

Regarding community camaraderie, today, I notice a difference in the interactional behavioral matrix of adults and children from the time of my childhood. Back then, people were visibly more neighborly. The adults in our block communicated and associated frequently. As a child, you had to go several blocks away if you wanted to engage in questionable activities. You would be "put in check" by an adult neighbor, and your parents would get a full report. We generally knew and associated with every adult and child living in our block. We played games with each other like "Hide and Go Seek," "Red Rover," "Four Squares," and my personal favorite, "catch a girl, kiss a girl." We went to the parks together and shared in birthday and block parties.

I recall an occasion when my mother got sick over the 4th of July holiday, which was her birthday. She had to be hospitalized for a couple of days. My mother discussed it with our next-door neighbor and me, and my three other siblings spent the night with her and her four children. After we moved into our current family home and began to mature into adolescence and adulthood, there was still camaraderie within the blocks and neighborhood. We formed baseball, basketball, and football teams that competed against other neighboring blocks. There was more of a sense of community, and gangbangers weren't an issue because we all grew up together and knew each other.

As a child in Chicago, there were primarily four gangs. Two were black (the Gangster Disciples, aka Disciples, aka the D's, and the Black P-Stone Nation, aka the Stones, who, from what I understand, had an affiliation with the Black Panther Party), one Latino (the Latin Kings) and one white (the Gaylords), who seemed to fizzle out for some reason. There wasn't much active engagement between them with the exception of an occasional clash between the D's and Stones. "Gangbanging" didn't seem to become a factor until the days of "Crack" cocaine. Today, those gangs don't exist, except for the Latin Kings. Today, they've evolved more into drug dealing clicks.

(Neighbors Behaviors)

Today, in the same block, I don't see the children at all and I reside in a dead-end street. I only know a couple neighbors from families whose children inherited the homes from their parents. A fairly recent family, whom I have difficulty calling neighbors because it implies friendliness, moved next door, initiated a feud, and, according to my mother, threatened to "kill" her! My mother was old enough to be her grandmother. I easily have 15 or 20 years on the woman myself. After my mother's passing in 2020, I tried developing a cordial relationship with them when I came to check on the house by saying hello and good morning, etc.… She would retort with a snort as if she were a horse.

Although I'm basically private and reserved by nature, I'm a friendly person and usually get along with everybody. I became aware of the tension between my mother and the people next door. Mother was tough and unforgiving if you managed to get on her bad side. However, I was willing to let bygones be bygones and wipe the slate clean. But I don't kiss ass either, and personally, she has an overabundance of the worst type in the category, and from every perspective you view her from, her shape can only be described as an oval. I'll try and take the high road and refrain from any further disgusting descriptions.

She chose to make it a family feud by allowing her unleashed dogs to venture into our yard to poop and scratch up the turf, as some dogs are known to do. Dogs are creatures of habit and tend to mark their territory. My mother had previously told me the woman had been doing this. My mother's lifetime hobby was working in the yard even before our house was built, she kept the yard well-manicured. She raised us to work in the yard, and I call myself "a cultivated Green Thumb." I suggested to mother to get evidence using her cell phone's camera/video app, and I showed her how to operate it.

Today, young folk call me "old school," so I classified my mother as "ancient school." She basically used her cell phone to call her children, which primarily was me to take her to get her gardening needs, grocery shopping, and to her doctor's appointments, etc.... She still had the same number to her landline phone since the house was built in 1973 and insisted I call her on it every day. After my mother's death and my eventual move into the property, the women then began lying and calling the police on me for trivial matters. And every time she called, she caught herself up in her own web of lies. Mother always said, "The truth don't change."

One summer day, as I was attempting to do some repairs on the backyard fence, she let her dogs out the front again. I pulled my cell phone out to get evidence for myself because these acts were regular. When I got to the front, her two small "ankle biter" dogs came after me in my yard, and due to the constant vertigo I experienced resulting from the stroke I suffered and the fact that I was unaware the hand-sized sledgehammer was not secure at the anvil, it fell off as I swung at the dogs, causing me to lose my balance and fall in the yard. After the incident, I went in the side door to get a drink of water and left the hammer on our blocked-glass window ledge.

As I stepped inside to get some bottled water, which took me all of six steps to the cabinet, twist the cap off, and start drinking, I heard a distracting sound that drew my attention to the block glass window and saw a silhouette's movement. I immediately went to the door and looked to the front of the gangway and saw the last part of her butt stepping up onto her one-stepped ledge leading to her front door. I then stepped out to the front but she had just closed the door behind herself.

I went back a few steps to get my hammer to continue my work and it was missing! I immediately went back to the front where she was now partially in and out of her doors with her left arm hidden behind the inner door. I then asked her to give me my hammer. She lied and said she didn't have it. Nobody else was around. She was acting as if common sense didn't apply. So I called the police. While I waited for them to come, she threatened to shoot and kill me three or four times (she's a uniformed security guard), then said she'd have her boyfriend handle me. Now I knew exactly where my mother was coming from!

By the time the two female police finally arrived, she had planted herself on her one-step ledge. They seemed to be heading toward her so I stepped outside and told them I was the one who had called and began telling them what happened. She interrupted me frequently and lied, saying I went into her yard and attacked her "dog," hitting it on the paw with the hammer. She also said she had video surveillance around her house. I demanded she show the tapes, which she refused. I then told them I had visual proof of her unleashed "dogs" doing their business in my yard. However, the police said this particular issue was about the theft of my hammer. Then she said, "Did you see me take it?" So, the police asked me about visual proof, and I told them what you just read and mentioned the common sense part of it all.

They did nothing to address the fact that she threatened my life several times and stated I didn't have actual visual proof that she had taken my hammer. Common sense ain't common these days. I later figured out where the lie that I hit "the dog" on the paw came from. When she stepped her oval ass inside the house, the "dogs" had to be at her side. The anvil must have fallen off the handle again, hitting one of the dogs on the paw. I call it common sense.

Once again, she talked too much, and her lies caught up with her. She blurted out that she kept her "dogs" on leashes. The police saw her as the aggressor, with me never having to show any of the pictures or videos I had in my phone. I was given paperwork backing up my claims of property damage/destruction. Since that event, I've continued collecting additional audio/visual proof as additional evidence for the court. This includes property destruction with her vehicles parked above the curb and onto the grass of my front yard of the curb. I learned technically, that's City property. With that being the case, I've always wondered why "the City" doesn't come and cut that part of the grass and why citizens pay taxes on it!

I won't bore you with all the stories, including interactions with her burly, oversized teenage son, who literally looks like he could be the real-life mascot for the Chicago Bears. All the petty interactions between us were totally uncalled for, avoidable, and pathetic. It's difficult to practice the "Golden Rule" or turn the other cheek with them for what you will read more about in the following subtitle. I must share two other short stories that delayed my writing and completion of the book for about 2 months in total. I'm contemplating taking them to court for the second reason I'm about to review.

The first delay resulted from my initially attempting to "voice text" the book to my e-mail on my phone. I intended to send it to publishers in small and specific sections. I soon learned that after a certain point, I was unable to continue updating my writing after I stopped for the day, so I had to copy and paste the entire draft before I could continue my writing.

Within a short time, I had at least 30 drafts of updated writing. So I deleted all of them except the most current and up-to-date version, which was roughly 30 pages of 8x11 sheets. When I went to review that single draft, aside from the title, it was blank! After about a week of depression, I began my rewrite on my laptop. 25 pages or so into the new draft, I went back and checked that old email draft, and lo' and behold, all the information had reappeared. I then began to reconcile the new 25 pages with what I had previously written. I felt the new writing was very good but that the original writing was more passionate. This took roughly another 2 weeks to reconcile.

(This Will Be The Day That I Die)

The second delay occurred because I was attacked and beaten by the people living next door. I recounted my mother's complaint and my suggestion she use her cell phone to capture images. I mentioned her threats to shoot and kill me and getting her six-something-over 250-pound boyfriend to "handle" all 5'6" of me with my notifying the police, resulting in paperwork and my obtaining additional audio/visual documentation.

In late February of 2022, she engineered a sneak attack on me as I was returning from the recycling dumpster. She blocked me by holding her door open and stepping onto my gangway (because we have kissing gangways) and started an argument. Then her boyfriend, who was hiding, jumped out of the house and, grabbed me by the throat and started choking me. I grabbed him by the throat and saw his eyes begin to bug out. Seeing this, oval ass hit me in my side, causing me to lose my breath and stomped on my left knee, causing me to lose my grip on his throat, and knocked me to the ground, where he began pulverizing my face and head as she stomped on my knee causing ligament damage and subsequent knee surgery. I thought I was going to die that day!

By the way, she's a beast, I mean obese. Since the assault, I've experienced certain anxiety about going outside when I see "her" vehicle that he drives present. Now I carry a metal pipe in my book bag when I leave home or to empty the garbage even. Legal action is in order for the attack because I incurred the costs for additional medical exams hospitalization costs, not to mention the property damage. However, I've experienced financial difficulties since having the stroke with its related medical costs and because I alone paid for my mother's funeral services (which, fortunately, she did, leave me monies to handle).

I'm currently in search of a pro bono attorney, and I haven't decided whether or not to put photos of the assault in the "AFTERWORDS." They are pretty grotesque, even though much of the swelling had gone down by the time the photos were taken 8 hours after the assault. I had to undergo CAT scans, MRI tests, and Ocular examinations because of white pearly flashes of light I still experience as of the writing. I had knee examinations for which a partial reconstruction was eventually performed, repairing my ACL, and as of May 2022, I'm undergoing Rehabilitation on my left knee. The 14-block ambulance ride to the hospital alone cost nearly $2000. The stroke of 2018 affected and weakened the left side of my body, again causing me to suffer from vertigo ever since.

(School Fool)

We all have our strengths and weaknesses. Nobody's perfect or knows everything. You could be 90 years old and still be naïve or ignorant about some things. Often, we learn of our naïveté the hard way, as I did while teaching in the Chicago Public Schools. Most likely, you've come across individuals who are competitive in everything they do. I'm not one of those people. I'm the type who tries my best at whatever I'm doing and understands I'm not always the cream of the crop. I don't compete against others except in sports and games. However, it would be boring if we were all created the same. I feel we're all created equal or equally, yet uniquely independent.

Some fail to realize there's always somebody "better" than you, even if you're considered an expert. Sometimes, you could be that big fish in a small pond. However, some people simply don't like you for whatever reason(s). I've learned that these "haters" and those overly competitive types can be some of the most envious and jealous backstabbing people on earth. I, like many others, have learned the hard way that these types will often smile in your face, then stab you in your back and undermine you at every opportunity. The sad thing is you may not be aware of their attitude, or worse, they could share your heritage or be considered a friend or family member.

For consecutive years, I interviewed for the band director's position with the Principal and department chairperson at Chicago's then only School for the Arts. They both shared my heritage. I didn't get the job initially, but the same position became available the next year. I interviewed again with the same people and got the job. I learned the department chair, and I attended the same high school. He graduated a couple years ahead of me but was never in the Band program.

When I inherited the program, it was in shambles. I was the third band director in 4 years for some students and the third director in 3 years for others. The numbers in the city's only "fine arts school" program had fallen to under 30 band students. In fact, when I taught at the elementary level, I sent many of my students to the school and attended their concerts on a regular basis.

Because I was able to recruit students from the All City Elementary Band program and was "required" to "work" my 1st & 2nd "prep" periods without additional compensation at a Baccalaureate Elementary School three blocks away (which is likely why my predecessors left), I rebuilt the program up to 85 strong playing students within 5 years. In a twist that eliminated the school's "Fine Arts" status, I switched elementary schools because the "Baccalaureate School" students could only participate in the band program for just the first semester of their freshmen year. The second school was significantly further requiring me to drive, but it became our school's primary neighborhood feeder school. From there, things went from bad to worse.

(Haters)

I was unaware I was being undermined by the music chairperson the entire time, and because of his disdain for me, he convinced the new Principal, who also graduated from our high school, to change my position from band director to beginning piano class for the next 5 years. The chairperson replaced me with someone of his choosing who no longer was "required to volunteer" his 1st & 2nd prep periods. In fact, he redesigned the 1st & 2nd periods for the Advanced Band, which was the Marching Band in the fall, and the Concert Band after the Christmas/New Year's Holiday season.

I also had to work after school, without pay, to rehearse the marching band. Traditionally, anyone working an after-school program was compensated. After teaching piano for 5 years, the full department realized I only had one lesson plan to prepare, and the chairperson decided to give me the last beginning band class of the day. Because of how the music periods were scheduled, by the time my class came around, there weren't sufficient working instruments to cover the class because a significant amount of instruments had fallen into disrepair due to the school's status change, which eliminated the luxury of having the "only" position of "instrument repairman" in the city.

This began the worst period in my life and teaching career. The school also got a new Principal, who I wrote about earlier, who confessed her lesbian lifestyle upon introducing herself to the faculty. For the first time in the school's history, the department didn't have sufficient instruments for an instrumental music class. This became a major obstacle and challenge. I had no choice but to adjust and engage the class from a rhythmic perspective by putting most students on percussion instruments, which wasn't the first choice for most.

With the school now officially a "neighborhood" school, the student racial breakdown, which was previously fairly evenly distributed, became about 60 percent Hispanic, with the remaining population split amongst Asian, Black, and White students. This new Administration instituted a policy that all student violations would be reported through the computer and handled solely by her administrative team. Although "artists" are said to be temperamental, from my experience, instrumental students learn to work together.

Soon, however, I began hearing racial slurs being spewed towards each other on a daily basis by the Hispanic segment of the class. They were calling each other the "N-word!" Although the slurs weren't directed at me, I was still offended and filed complaints on a nearly daily basis. In fact, an assistant principal, who was given charge over disciplinary actions, approached me in April and said, "I hear you loud and clear, and you need not submit any more write-ups." However, there were no detentions, suspensions, or parent conferences regarding the racial slurs I was hearing daily. My complaints had fallen on deaf ears because he made no corrective disciplinary efforts.

In his final year before he retired, the department chair set the schedule for the next year and arranged for me to teach the Intermediate band class.

Again, for the first time in the school's history, he programmed the vast majority of the former beginning band students to skip Intermediate band and go directly to Advanced band. I knew it was because of his disdain for me and because of the fact the band's student numbers, in general, had plummeted again.

This was after all the hard work and sacrifices I made to rebuild the program.

This left me with the students who weren't really interested in band, with most being from my previous Beginning Band class for this Intermediate group. The department chair, working with his "groomed" incoming chairperson, seemed to convince enough disinterested beginning students to hang in there for an additional year. Again, it was the last class of the day, and there weren't enough quality instruments to serve the students. Another first in the school's history occurred! That particular Intermediate Band was unable to perform at the annual winter and spring concerts or at the City and State music festivals.

By this time, the misuse of cell phones had become an issue in the school system. The students' overuse of them became a distraction in the classroom, affecting the teacher's ability to have a focused student body to instruct. The second-year Principal adopted a vague policy that stated students could use phones in the halls between classes and in the cafeteria. With her policy, each teacher had the discretion to state their class policy as either a red or green phone zone, representing non-usage or permission to use them. This led to the incident I wrote about at the top of the book under the title.

To set up the incident, I was at the band room door between classes, monitoring and welcoming my students into the class and out of the halls, when Alex came towards the class with earbuds on and plugged into his phone. As he approached me and we made eye contact, I motioned to him to remove his earbuds. Although my class had already been a designated a "Red Zone," this was a usual request, and students always complied.

As he walked past me, entering the band room, I saw him plugging back in. I called out to him but he either ignored me or didn't hear me. Believing the buds to be too loud, I followed behind him and naturally increased my voice volume, asking him a second, then a third time to remove the buds. About that time, another student got his attention, signaling him to remove the equipment as my voice was peaking with my request. That was when the incident occurred…

As I had seen this kid previously around school before being placed in my class, I observed him to be the quiet loner type. He seemed to make friends with the two girls he sat between in the flute section directly in front of me. They became downright talkative and did very little to learn and grow on their instrument, so I was totally stunned when he exploded on me as he did. I was told he was placed in detention for the rest of the day.

Again, the school's "administrative team" initiated no interaction or dialogue with his parent(s) and me. I was, on the other hand, written up, and an official reprimand was entered into my record because I was prepared to fight him and returned a racial slur with profanity, especially after he said, "That's why your mother sucks yo' daddy's nasty ass dick!" After a few days, they switched him to another class. If I were to profile a student, he would've been the type to bring a gun to school and mow me down along with others in the process.

At this point, I was in my 23rd year of service. All of them, except one had been at schools that were predominantly Latino. In all that time, I maybe heard the word "Nigger" 3 or 4 times. Each time I shut the class down and had an open discussion about the hurtfulness of racial slurs. I was able to name racial slurs used against Black, White, Hispanic and Asian populations. I never heard the slur twice in any class or in back-to-back years until the beginning of this 3-year, most hellacious period of my teaching career.

Chapter: 2

AMERICA...
...I AM RACE

(The Race To Inequality)

I'm not sure when or where I first learned that the letters in "AMERICA" reconfigured spelled "I AM RACE," but I've known it for decades. The only other person I heard make reference to it was recently deceased comedian Paul Mooney on a YouTube video a couple years ago saying something to the effect that it was "coded in." The point being I can't take credit for originally deciphering it. However, when I've shared this fact with others, with the exception of a 3rd cousin, I've yet to meet anyone who was aware of it.

The word "Race" has a dual meaning. One having to do with ethnicity, describing groups of humans based on shared physical differences and cultures considered socially significant. Ethnicity refers to a shared culture, such as language, ancestry, practices, and beliefs. The other meaning of "Race" refers to a competition of getting from one place to another quicker or faster than something or someone else, usually in a contest or adversarial context.

It requires "beating them" to be declared the winner, the best, number one, or "Top Dog," and claiming its inherent bragging rights. Depending on the nature of the race, it could demonstrate levels of savvy, skill, strength, cunningness, and/or deception. It's my opinion both definitions have combined and morphed themselves into the fabric of this country to become uniquely the "American Way." I view these intertwined definitions as being connected to a financial aspect as well.

When I combine the two definitions for America, it insinuates one ethnicity beating all other ethnicities to, therefore, "win" or rule the country, thus negating the "Democratic process." America is a multi-racial/ethnic country, which is supposedly one of its strengths. A Republic based on democracy that declares it is "of, for and by the people" and where the majority (of the people) rule. Not "of, for, and by the race or ethnicity," or where race rules. This would imply that each race or ethnic group is already preprogrammed to think, feel, and react exactly the same at all times, having no individuality or diversity and is predictable. This is a disgusting and revolting assumption of thought and would be stereotyping at the highest level, aka Hitler and the Aryan race.

Exactly what is the American form of government? I've heard it called a Democracy, a Republic, a Democratic Republic, and a Constitutional Republic. In a "Democracy," laws are made directly by a voting majority, leaving the rights of the minority largely unprotected. In a "Republic," laws are made by "Representatives" chosen by the people, who are supposed to comply with a constitution that specifically protects the rights of the minority from the will of the majority.

Let's look at the Pledge of Allegiance and what we're pledging to. The third and current rendition of 1954 states: "I pledge allegiance to the Flag of the United States of America, and to the Republic for which it stands, one nation under God, indivisible, with liberty and justice for all." The original Pledge stated: "I pledge allegiance to my Flag and the Republic for which it stands, one nation, indivisible with liberty and justice for all." Then came some revisions in 1923 that I once heard recited in the movie "Bright Road," an all Black casted movie featuring Harry Belafonte as the school's Principal and Dorothy Dandridge as the classroom teacher.

As I tried to reconcile these ideas of democracies and Republics, majorities and minorities, I formed the following conclusions, so hang in here with me for this roller coaster ride. We don't pledge allegiance to the people or our country or to the Constitution, but to a "flag" and to the idea of a

"Republic." Based on the previous definitions, the Republic are the people "we elect as Representatives" and who are the actual "true minority" of the people in the country. They then decide laws for the rest of us, based on "their" interpretation of what "they" think we want, then promise or pledge it all to a flag and an idea called "The Republic," which is actually "themselves" and not to you and me the people aka the public!

Whew! That's a lot to take in, and I'm still confused. So, in trying to understand where I fit in all this and what "our" (meaning the people's) general collective standing is, for what it's worth, our country, "the Republic," is supposed to protect the minorities' interest, aka our elected officials. This makes it clear why we, the people (the majority), seldom get what we want because this "true minority," aka our elected officials, seems to always get their way. Elected officials do, however, swear a solemn oath to uphold the Constitution.

Permit me to interject this point. When I say "our elected officials," the people of my heritage weren't always allowed to vote and are still having problems doing it as recently as the 2020 election with the gerrymandering that occurred for example at North Carolina A&T University, the largest HBCU in the country, where the campus itself was gerrymandered, taking away their one "Black" Representative by boldly and blatantly splitting the campus itself and that district's vote into two "White" districts and Representatives.

As I will repeatedly make reference to America, your cruel and repressive actions against the people of my heritage have never let up. There was the opportunity to right the wrongs of slavery during the Reconstruction era. However, when we look back and analyze what occurred, history documents a continuous series of landmark economic and political laws (enacted by "our" elected officials), various statutes, and (Supreme) court cases that affect the people of my heritage to this very day (RSWS: 1, 2, 3, 4, 5, 6, 7, 8 & 9).

Is this a reason some people don't want history taught and try and radicalize it into the catchphrase "Critical Race Theory?" Is history required to make people feel comfortable or uncomfortable? I say no. It's simply the facts. The people pushing against a truthful narrative reminds me of a now-famous catchphrase line from the movie "A Few Good Men" of "You can't handle the truth!" And some obviously can't! The question remains, why can't they?

It seems that when the country takes a step forward, inevitably, it takes several steps backward. The people of my heritage are literally no better off today than we were following the abruptly shortened period of Reconstruction, which after nearly 250 years of enslavement was nipped in the bud after roughly only 10 years as a result of backroom dealings during the election to the presidency of Rutherford B. Hayes where "the Party of Lincoln" northern Republicans (Repunkicans), ensured the Southern white Democrats (Dumasscraps) and former slaveholders of their continued economic dominance, so as to "not offend them." For example, if you look at today's family household income equality gap, for which I will examine shortly, it alone speaks for itself, with this being around 160 years later.

Earlier, I referenced a saying I've heard in my community of "change the game in the game," made evident in the example of the Repunkican Party denying President Obama his constitutional right to select a Supreme Court Justice by first circumventing Senate rules and Constitutional law and by that denial, stole one, then inserted 2 more "lying" Supreme Court Justices or rather "Injustices." Well, there's another saying I've heard that goes, "White people make a plan, then they work that plan." Made evident in stacking the Supreme Court, in the manner they did, as part of their 50-year "long game" plan to undermine abortion rights, aka Roe v Wade (and by implication other rights), against what the majority of people feel in the country on that issue. I'm not debating the pros and cons of abortion in this reading, just the ugly political game of how others impose their often "minority" views on the majority. However, on this particular issue, the "minority view" was still protected in that no one was "forcing you" to have an abortion!

To interpret the ideas of progression versus digression, as I understand this topic and as discussed in my circles, it's "Their" plan (certain white folk) to maintain a chokehold on their existing power structure by "any means necessary." In other words, it means to change whatever rule(s) or law(s) to maintain their grip on power via "change the game in the game."

And if that fails, it means simply to take the ball and go home, or leave the country without anything to play with. In other words, to end this "Experiment in Democracy." Some (particularly White) people have amassed so much wealth that they and their posterity can go to their ancestral countries of origin and live more than comfortably for generations to come. Whereas the ancestral lineage of the people of my heritage, for the most part, has been severed.

(Then Add Some Strife To The Mix)

As mentioned in the introduction, this book easily could have been entitled "Born To A Life Of Strife." As I delved into the word "Race," now I will visit the word "Strife." Because of your RACE, you're born into and subjected to a lifetime of "STRIFE!" How fair is that? Having to live an unjustified lifetime of snarky, stressful torment. That's a big pill to swallow. To examine the word and its intentions, a Google search of it in its **Merriam-Webster Dictionary since 1828** defines Strife as (1) a lack of agreement or harmony. (2) An earnest effort for superiority or victory over another. This second definition is eerily reminiscent of the definition of "Race."

Again, I find both definitions applicable. In the first, obviously, there was a lack of agreement between the enslaver and the enslaved. It's inconceivable those newly enslaved people agreed to living under conditions that would cause them to be subservient, abused, beaten and raped, etc.... Neither did their millions of offspring born into bondage make any such agreement, nor were they given the opportunity to choose.

Would any one of you reading this chose to be enslaved?

We all know the answer. I don't like having to live with many racial conditions I'm confronted with today, which pales by comparison to that of being enslaved. However, it's the second definition that fits so snuggly in the America I'm discussing in this book, "An earnest effort for superiority or victory over another," where the enslaver claimed superiority over the enslaved by discounting their humanity. This country is replete with examples of this, for example, quantifying the enslaved as 3/5 or 60% of a man. I heard somewhere how they came up with that ratio, but it's still beyond me and lends itself, in my opinion, to their cunning selfishness and/or mental illness. They also discounted the Native people's humanity by labeling them "Savages."

"There is a physical difference between the white and black races which I believe will forever forbid the two races from living together... while they do remain together, there must be a position superior and inferior, and I am as much as any man in favor of having the superior position assigned to the white race."(10)

Abraham Lincoln

Most of us evolve and change over time as we get new information. What we might think or say at one stage in our lives could very well change as we become more informed or enlightened. So, should something a person said in elementary school be held against them when they are 50 years old? It could be taken out of context. It would depend on the consistency of behaviors and actions one would have made during those intervening years. Here is a clipping from a letter to Horace Greenley from Abraham Lincoln, dated Friday, Aug 22, 1862.

"If I could save the Union without freeing any slave, I would do it, and if I could save it by freeing all the slaves, I would do it, and if I could save it by freeing some and leaving others alone, I would do that."(11)

Abraham Lincoln

The last statement was made significantly into his presidency. Therefore, I have difficulty calling Abraham Lincoln a hero of mine because he was "wishy-washy" on his stance regarding "the equality reality of humanity." In my opinion, JOHN BROWN was a true American hero because he fought and died for the equality reality of humanity during the most repulsive and disgusting enslavement period of the country. I feel he was a real man of integrity, and his undeterred conviction to the truth, is sorely missing today in the American Congress, in many people in the country and around the world in general.

Although the science was known to the "enlighten founders" of this country regarding the equality reality of humanity and what was considered human, the enslaved were made to feel less than that and intellectually inferior, as if they were some kind of hybrid livestock. They were labeled "Chattel" and considered incapable of self-directed governance. This was how enslavers laid the foundation for their economic dominance and victory over them.

I believe this a part of the current Repunkican systemic philosophical justification and reasoning for protesting some Colleges and Universities teaching the "1619 project," aka Critical Race Theory (CRT) or, as I call it, "a part of basic US history." Also, the curriculum, contrary to the misinformation and fear-mongering being spewed, is NOT being taught in any K-12 municipality in the country. If so, I'm not aware of it.

While on the topic of US History being taught in schools, a few years ago, while still teaching, I had an opportunity to browse through some old history books that were being discarded. I looked in the index for the word slavery. It showed only a single page. Then, I looked up the chapter on the Civil War. It had several pages, with one page on slavery being the last page of the chapter. Then it dawned on me it was also the shortest chapter in the entire book.

When I turned to the one page on slavery, the script didn't take up the entire page. The top half was a cartoonish drawing of an enslaved woman outdoors sweeping, which reminded me of the lady on the old "Aunt Jemima Syrup" bottle because of her smiling, full, robust cheeks and the scarf tied over her head. It looked like an exact copy of the woman on the bottle! They portrayed her as jovial and seemingly content.

Fairly recently, the company changed that stereotypical facial caricature. The drawing was followed by two short paragraphs. C'mon now! Was that the sum total of the enslavement period in America? That's an example of extreme historical inaccuracy by writing only two measly paragraphs for roughly 250 years of enslavement. Not even the "traditional" drawn ship with the enchained humans "packed in like sardines" that depicted the Middle Passage voyage across the Atlantic was present. Liar, liar, pants on fire!

I diverged. Returning to strife and my previous train of thought, while writing in this chapter, I sat and thought for a moment, then easily came up with an acronym for the word STRIFE as it relates to this book and my experience. You will note that an alternate one sprang forth as well, and common to them both is the word "Racism."

S....Systemic............................. Systematic.....S
T...Tormenting............................Torturous.....T
R...Racism................................Racism.....R
I....Infused...............................Injected.....I
F....For................................... Frequently.....F
E...Everything............................Everyday.....E

There's a long list of synonyms for the word "Strife," with some being self-inflicted within our communities. However, I'm reminded that much of it was constructed and implanted by design and originated with the "Willie Lynch Letter." That's not to say it never would've occurred without that influence because "Strife" occurs worldwide. Some synonyms include: Argue, altercation, battle, bicker, clash, conflict, disunity, division, enmity, fighting, friction, grapple, hassled, infighting, ill will, quarreling, rivalry, squabble, schism, variance, and warring. This unrelenting Strife was introduced to the people who share my heritage from the very beginning of our interactions with the colonial Europeans.

(The "Golden Rule" Don't Work, So, I Offer You...)

"Do unto others as you would have them do unto you" is called the "Golden Rule." Essentially, it's the (last six) commandments of the "Law of Moses" in the Old Testament of the Holy Bible (King James version). The intent is to treat your neighbor, meaning everyone you interact with, the way you'd want them to treat you. In my lifetime of observation, I generally don't see it practiced. In practical reality, it doesn't seem to work! The few who do practice it are usually taken advantage of because most people take their kindness for weakness (aka, nice guys finish last).

The way I see it, we tend not to see the three fingers pointing back at ourselves when we so easily see and point out the flaws and faults of others. Again, I believe we generally try to do and say the right things, especially if we participate in a faith-based religion and sincerely strive to be of a "Godlike" mindset. I don't know anybody who likes criticism, whether it's constructive or not, and I feel people want to be correct every time on everything they do.

No one except true psychopaths or sociopaths purposefully do wrongful acts. I'm not saying that people haven't planned crimes, and I'm sure that all of us have, at some point, had the thought to "get even" with someone who has done us wrong, especially if we felt it was done on purpose. Neither am I saying that anybody is without sin and hasn't done some dirt. Nobody's perfect, right? Still, I've heard it said that some people don't think their poo poo stinks.

As I have learned through religious studies, the educational process, and from personal observation, historically, throughout the centuries, the clergy has been, at best, inconsistent or "Sometimey." Sometimes the Church says, "My brother's keeper." Sometimes it's been, "Slave obey thy master." Sometimey! A current example is how the "White Evangelical Clergy" Church community, including "White Christian Nationalists organizations," have cuddled up to former president Donald $kunk, with his blatant, outrageous comments and behaviors, his constant lying and perverse degradation of women, the physically handicapped, other minorities and the people of my heritage.

When I observed his outright contempt for athletes taking a knee (which is actually a sign of humility) and other people of color worldwide, as well as his comments and mistreatment of immigrants, especially their children, of whom the Bible calls "The Strangers In Your Land," and "the least us," it forces my common sense to make assessments and draw conclusions.

Unfortunately, we are all forced to make evaluations and judgments on the character of others. If a person gets caught stealing, they're judged to be a thief. A School Teacher has to judge everyday. Be that as it may, as it relates to the former president's actions, you have to ask, is that something Buddha, Moses, Jesus, or Mohammed would have condoned or condemned?

Do you think they would have cuddled up to those types of actions and behaviors? The former president awarded a huge tax cut to the wealthiest 1% of our population and corporations, thereby placing a greater tax burden on the poor. Jesus admonishes us to be considerate of the poor. Do you think "The Lord" would have called him out for what he has shown himself to be? A tree is known by its' fruit, and we all witnessed the fruit of former president "Skunk." IT STUNK!

The callousness he demonstrated on a daily basis towards nearly everyone and particularly to the "least of them," aka the children, was an example of an evil and hardened heart. Some might call it demonic or sociopathic. And with him never being called out or rebuked by the primarily white "Evangelical Christians" or their clergy, I assess them to be the modern-day "Pharisees and Sadducees," of whom Jesus rebuked and overturned their money tables.

I call them "Hypocrite Christians" with hearts of stone, devoid of the LOVE of GOD, or any type of Christian Love, and to whom I've labeled "HYPOCHRISTIANS!!!" Where was the "Golden Rule" being applied? Where is the "Golden Rule" being applied now? They are so easily tossed "to and fro."

The time to stand up was then and also now! There is a well-known saying that states, "If you don't stand for something, you will fall for anything," and these "Evangelicals" are another group who have done just that and, in the process, causing many to question "Christianity" in general. Actually, I don't think they were "falling for anything." More accurately, I believe it to be simply going along with the lies and the Bu!!$#!+. Am I correct in assessing the Golden Rule wants you to treat "somebody" and, by extension, all the peoples of the world the way you want that same "somebody" to treat you in return? Wouldn't that be fair to say?

(..."The Bronze Rule")

Hence, I give you "The Bronze Rule." It states, rather than "Do unto others," says, "I'll do unto you the way you do unto me." I'll treat you the way you treat me. In other words, people should treat YOU the way you treat THEM. With this, you'd quickly learn how you treated someone else by getting instant feedback and results. I realize many would call it "an eye for an eye." Again, I would like to add my two cents and say, on the flip side, you'd also have the first opportunity to initiate Goodwill then have it returned back onto you. How would you like that? Do you think former president Skunk would like it? Have you heard the saying that: "Fair is fair, just is just, and right is right?" But is it? Not from what I've witnessed! It hasn't shown itself to be that. What I've observed is:

Fair is not fair
Just is not just
And
Right is White...!
Have you heard this saying before?
If you're White, you're all right.
If you're Yellow, you're mellow.
If you're Brown, stick around.
If you're Black, get back.
The Nile Valley Contributions to Civilizations: pg. 26
By: Anthony Browder
But I say: It seems that...
If you're White, you're right.
If you're Light, you're all right.
If you're Yellow, you're mellow.
If you're Brown, stick around.
If you're Black, get back.
And I also add,
If you're Red, you're Dead!

In this country, not all have been shown the fairness, justice, and righteousness afforded to some. On MSNBC's "The Rachel Maddow Show" in…2021, during one of her reports, she brought to the forefront two cases of 2020 election voter fraud. One case was the intentional actions of a lady who shares my heritage, where she purposely sent in a mail-in ballot and forged the signature of her 12-year deceased mother.

The other case involved a white man who, in an unintentional act of ignorance, was not aware of the voter restriction laws of his State related to his previous felony incarceration. He was then directed by an election official to cast a provisional ballot that wasn't actually counted!

The women received the proverbial "slap on the wrist" of probation. The man got the proverbial "hammer dropped" on him. He got an excessive amount of jail time and was sentenced to serve five additional years of imprisonment! Now, was that fair, just, or right?

Oops! I got the storylines mixed up…!

In fact, it was just the reverse, whereas the white man had sent in the mail-in ballot with the intentionally forged signature of his 12-year deceased mother and got the proverbial slap on the wrist of probation, and the black woman who unknowingly cast the uncounted provisional ballet receiving the excessive amount of jail time! Again, I ask you the same question. Was it fair, just, or right? Florida's Governor, Ron DeSantis, is openly guilty of the same practices with the same racial breakdowns. Is that fair, just, or right?

Then there's Jenna Ryan! I saw a story about her blatant and arrogant pronouncement of her white privilege on CBS DFW on 11/14/21, where she openly proclaimed, "I got blonde hair, and I'm white. I'm definitely not going to jail." Only because her comments generated such a level of outrage captured on social media did, she end up pleading guilty to her participation in the Capitol riot/insurrection and served only 60 days in jail with a $1,500 fine.

Was that true justice for trying to overthrow the government and this country? The Confederate army didn't even do what they did! When you look at the penalties for breaking these types of laws, the sentences and fines could've been much more severe. She and others wanted to overthrow the free and fair election and this country's government for their own selfish purposes. Just forget about what's right, just or fair!

Contrast that with the Black Panther Party of the 1960s. While exercising their currently much talked about "2nd Amendment Rights" and acting on the lawful open carry provision, where they were monitoring and protecting their community from the influx of criminal activities, including drug trafficking and the terrorizing intimidation of neighborhood gangs. They made possible breakfast meals for children, other educational and after-school programs, political registration, and other uplifting "self-initiative" programs within their community.

While minding their business within their own community and after being infiltrated by a "plant" from Hoover's FBI, they were attacked and slaughtered, with their leadership and family members gunned down in the privacy of own residences by government agents. This reminds me of a more recent incident involving Breonna Taylor, the innocent young lady murdered in her residence by police in Louisville, KY.

In another fairly recent case, there was Clive Owens, who had trained snipers aiming weapons at federal agents because "He" decided "He" wanted to confiscate federally protected lands for himself. No violent encounter occurred! Not one shot was fired. Was that fair? Where is the justice? Contrast that to the Black Panthers, who never trained their guns on federal agents or police. Their guns were for protection if they were attacked, in accordance with their 2nd amendment right. Yet they were decimated!

I heard about the sniper in Dallas being killed by a robotic bomb during a 2nd Amendment right-to-bear arms parade in May 2018. I had never heard of a sniper being killed like that before or since, and of course, he happened to be a man who shares my heritage. At the time, I recall police officials had falsely accused another individual of being that sniper as he participated in that parade in Dallas while the altercation was active. Is this another classic case of "all Black men look alike?"

Did this type of confusion happen in the Parkland High School shooting or in the historical Emanuel African Methodist Episcopal Church in Charleston, SC, or at the elementary school in Sandy Hook, Conn, when a gunman shot down 20 children and teaching personnel, or at the grocery store in Buffalo, NY, or the mass shooting in Las Vegas compared to the Uvalde, Texas shooting?

Then there were thousands of primarily White, with some Hispanic and Black participants (more on them later), from "the party of law and order," aka Republicans insurrectionists/seditionists deeply involved in attacking the US Capitol in Washington DC bashing, smashing and thrashing over and through "the people's" walls, halls, doors and windows, while smearing feces inside the building that seats our government and injuring over 140 Capitol police, DC Metropolitan police officers and other governmental enforcement protective personnel, in their attempt to overthrow our Constitutional Democratic Republic and install a psychotic dictator!

I can't speak for our Spanish-speaking community, but they always seem to find the "token" black(s) in incidents like this. However, upon further review of the revealed tapes surrounding the attack, I personally didn't see any people sharing my heritage actively participating in the events of that day.

The rioters sole intent was to inflict serious bodily harm and/or death onto the police officers and our duly elected officials and lynch the Vice President of these "United" States of America in their effort to prevent them from completing a "MERE FORMALITY" of an already officially certified process, aka the Presidential election, while some pledged allegiance to the "Confederate" flag and to Donald Skunk!

How many from this mob were arrested or killed at the time? Little to none! One "protester" died… That incident was pure Strife! Was it "fair" for them to do that? Were they acting on a "just" cause? Were they "right?" "Hell Nawl," and you can't tell me different!

Now we're learning that some of the then Congressional membership who spouted lies and conspiracy theories are some the very ones who encouraged and participated in setting it up. Look at "Jenny" Thomas, wife of Supreme Court "Justice" Clarence Thomas, for one example.

As a child, I remember my mother working in customer service for Sears (initially Sears & Roebuck. Roebuck was a black man). Some years later she was promoted to accounts receivable, where I'm guessing she got a pay increase. In total, she served Sears around 25 years. However, I remember her telling me how her bosses required her to regularly train the younger upstart white girls, usually fresh out of high school and all of whom were promoted over her into higher paying upper level management and supervisory positions.

In essence, they all became her bosses. Was that fair, just, or right? Was that the "Golden Rule" being enacted? However, it was a lot of STRESS, STRAIN, and STRIFE placed on my mother! I don't know if you've heard this saying before about the Golden Rule, but it goes, "HE WHO HAS THE GOLD RULES."

I'll try and keep this story brief involving a personal experience I had with the Golden Rule. After teaching for a number of years, I began buying a house that had a full but unfinished basement. I became very active musically and acquired an equipment setup of near studio quality and proportions, with the ability to host at least a 20-piece ensemble. I could've easily demanded a $50-75 per hour rental fee to use my facility had that been my mindset.

Over time, I began playing primarily with three groups, the first being the "Merchants," an 18-piece Jazz/R&B ensemble. Initially we rehearsed at the founder and bandleader Roland Brown's house, then at a park district field house. A couple years later, we gained a member (Jess Williams) who founded "Soundmine Studios," a Grammy award-winning recording facility. Jess allowed us to rehearse at the studio for free. He also recorded a CD with and for us with no expense to the membership.

A couple years later, Roland Brown died but had already passed the Baton on to me. A few years after that, Jess Williams fell ill and died, and the use of his facility became an expense. After his transition and a few rehearsals in my basement, the family again allowed us to rehearse freely as I negotiated the group add "Soundmine" to the Merchants" to always promote the studio, and I always take time during our performance to acknowledge these two gentlemen, who we also call and added to our list of ancestors.

So, In 2018, I suffered a stroke. Now unable to work and having to use my pension to pay off my bills and medical expenses pretty much exhausted my financial resources. Although still not at 100%, it's by the "Grace of God" I personally rehabbed the affected side of my body enough to be able to play once again. 2 years later, the COVID-19 pandemic hit.

About a month into the pandemic, my mother fell down her staircase and broke the bones in her throat, which then required her to fed via a tube placed directly into her stomach. It also required her to be monitored 24 hours a day or be placed in a nursing home, which she vehemently objected to. I was with her every day and night for the first two months after she fell, except for rehearsal times. This also prevented me from doing my "Uber Eats" side hustle, which had given me some cash influx.

The second group was a "combo." We initially rotated houses to avoid one person having to shoulder the cost of an excessive electricity bill and other inconveniences. Somehow, over a relatively short period of time, circumstances prevented the other members from hosting, and it all came down to using my basement. Because we initially rotated, we ever paid each other. I never thought to ask them for payment because I didn't find it to be a financial burden and I had it to freely give.

With the third group, we practiced free of charge for years in my basement. About a year after having the stroke and because my financial situation became desperate, I asked the group to pay $30 per month, which came out to a dollar and some change per week or 50-60 cent an hour. Some members were inconsistent with their payment. I often heard fully employed men with good jobs in the same profession as I had been saying, "I'll pay you next week." The point being I saw no application of the "Golden Rule" enacted on my behalf.

My mother died in the summer of 2020, and soon after that, I lost my house of 21 years and moved to our family house that following January. I'm not blaming any of them and perhaps I should have been more business savvy. Some membership carried over from one group to the next. However, there was no thought to provide me any assistance to lighten my load coming from any of them and they all were fully aware of my circumstance. With the big band and before the family allowed us to again rehearse at Soundmine Studios, I eventually requested a $2 per person rehearsal fee. I got the idea from another musician we all knew who had been charging that fee for rehearsals in his basement. We had one rehearsal before the pandemic hit and shut everything down.

Finally, the saying, "A friend in need is a friend indeed," is attributed to the Greek playwright Euripides back in 400 BC. As I mentioned earlier, after falling on hard times, I moved back to the family house after 21 years of buying. When making the move, I asked my best and oldest friend to assist with moving the smaller items because he had a work truck. The moving company handled the larger items. When it all said and done, I paid him as much, if not more than as I paid the entire three-man moving team.

He also asked for and received several additional perks for things he requested that I had, including some construction materials and tools he used in his line of work. He also asked for some lifting weights and a new Hewlett-Packard printer, still in its original packaging, that then cost around $1,000 for use in his independent construction business and for which I freely gave.

Then, roughly 7 months later, I asked him to write a letter for me to assist me in getting my utility bill costs reduced because I was literally financially broke. He made some excuse regarding to his writing skills, but he lived with a highly educated, newly retired woman. I reminded him of the additional gifts he asked for that I freely gave him and that writing the letter should be manageable.

I didn't hear from him again. It was nearly a year later, after one of his family members died, that he reached out and shared the unfortunate news. The point being is the "Golden Rule" doesn't seem to work. I have always been very generous with whatever I had at my disposal and freely willing to share and help make things happen and easy for others. The thought re-enters my mind that people most often seem to take kindness for weakness.

(...And All Of America Participated...)

Returning back to the slave trade and the continuous compounding levels of stress that were being levied upon my enchained and soon-to-be enslaved ancestors. They were packed into Middle Passage ships like sardines in a can, now headed for America, where they would be subjected to further humiliating scrutiny, inspections, and degradation. Once their bare feet hit the ground on these shores, the bound and chained, soon to be fully enslaved, were physically inspected. A potential slave buyer would perform a Hands-On inspection of these scantly clad and often naked people by touching, squeezing, poking, and prodding them from head to toe.

As stated previously, the enslaved were considered high-priced and valuable commodities. Contrary to popular belief, the slave trade wasn't exclusive to the southern states. In the early days of the budding enterprise, slaves were sold and traded on "Wall Street" at what is now the New York Stock Exchange (NYSE) in downtown Manhattan. I heard this was where the term "commodities" originated. In 2019, less than 2 blocks away, a small plaque was placed that acknowledges and commemorates the fact that over 400 years ago, the enslaved actually built the "original wall" of Wall Street.

The slave trade thrived under British and Dutch colonial rule in America. They used the enslaved to establish their farms and build their new towns and cities, as well as contrived deals to finance trips back to Akebulan for continuous enslavement. The triangular trade route, which started in Europe, sailed to Alkebulan, then to colonial America, the Caribbean Islands, and Central and South America before returning to Europe, was profitable for investors. It turned Capital markets in London by selling debt to ships, goods, and people. Northern US banks, namely New York Life, AIG, and Aetna, aligned with southern plantations by selling securities to help fund the expansion of plantations, to balance the risks involved with forcibly bringing humans from Akebulan, and to protect the risks involved in the possibilities of ships sinking and injuries to or the loss of the individuals enslaved.

There was an overflow of cash profits, and American Banks accepted the deposits. In New England, cotton from Southern plantations was sent to Massachusetts and Rhode Island and turned into fabric. In Boston, merchants made a profit by selling timber and ice to the South and Caribbean in return for cotton and sugar. Brooks Brothers turned cotton into high fashion. Domino Sugar refined sugar cane. The American railroads transported goods on lines initially built by the enslaved. What is now JP Morgan Chase Bank subsidized Citizens Bank and the Canal Bank of Louisiana and accepted slaves as collateral for loans and took ownership if they defaulted. (12)

Fast forward to 1865, to the northern city and Capitol of the United States, Washington DC, just after the death of Abraham Lincoln. America had just fought a Civil War against herself and recognized her demons and the unjustness of what is called the "original sin" of slavery. I personally add to this original sin to include not only the theft of human lives but also of the theft of the lands of the Indigenous people. Nevertheless, America now has the opportunity to heal and repair herself. To make right the wrongs she committed against a significant portion of her citizenship. This was her opportunity to make reparation to those formerly enslaved!

However, the southern-born slavery-loving Vice President Andrew Johnson is by law installed as president after Mr. Lincoln's assassination and immediately begins a campaign of squashing Reconstruction and any opportunity for "Reparations" to flourish under the guise of not wanting to alienate "White Southerners" and former slaveholders, by first initiating the "Black Codes." I ask, is there any room for a conspiracy theory regarding the assassination of Mr. Lincoln? Within the very short period of roughly 10 years from 1867-1877, the "Reconstruction Act" itself is totally squashed out like kindling at a campfire as a result of backroom dealings and the "Gentlemen's agreement" that came to be known as the Compromise of 1877.

A Google search reveals the Compromise of 1877 was an "informal" agreement between Southern Democrats (Dimasscraps) and allies of Republican (Repunkican) Rutherford B. Hayes to settle the result of the 1876 presidential election, which marked the end of the Reconstruction Era.

The outcome of the election hinged largely on the disputed returns from Florida, Louisiana, and South Carolina, the only three states in the South with Reconstruction-era Republican governments still in power. Hayes' allies secretly met with "moderate" Southern Democrats and negotiated acceptance of Hayes' election. The Dumasscraps agreed not to block Hayes' victory on the condition that Repunkicans withdraw all federal troops from the South, which consolidated the Democrats control over the region and thereby officially ending Reconstruction.

I've drawn three conclusions as a result of this compromise. First, that although the two major political parties traditional roles have flip-flopped, it's amazing how, after roughly 150 years, the nicknames I gave them are still applicable today.

Secondly, the politics of American "backroom" dealings are a staple in this government (Ex. Republican backroom deals to deny President Obama Supreme Court judge selection of Merrick Garland and their passing of the tax cuts to the wealthiest 3% of the population, which was a huge part in what increased the national debt nearly 8 trillion dollars under former president Skunk administration).

Third, some things shouldn't be compromised, especially when it means being fair, just, and right with regard to human lives and the American citizenry. I also heard somewhere the main reason slavery was permitted to end was due to another of those backroom deals that guaranteed former slave-holders supervisory positions and control over contracts for reconstructing their damaged infrastructure and for the future construction related the continued building of a growing America in general.

(On The Backs of...)

At that point in time, especially in the South, white America wasn't used to building much of anything. Who did they use, cheat and pay less than a fair wage for their working labors? And from whom did they learn? Naturally, from the formerly enslaved! The historical record reveals he primarily used the formerly enslaved, particularly those who violated the so-called "Black Codes," which is the first proven form of entrapment and re-enslavement. Any white person could at any time claim a black person violated a "code" because their word was undisputed!

"Black Codes" were unofficial "petty laws" and rules instituted during the Andrew Johnson regime that were designed to keep newly freed slaves "in their place" by first legislating, then enforcing ridiculous laws, like, for example, not looking white people directly in their eyes or having to cross the street when approaching them and time curfews forcing black folk off the streets by certain times, that when violated, would cause the imprisonment of the formerly enslaved, which most frequently happened to the men and became another means of separating them from their families.

Once the formerly enslaved were jailed, they could be "rented or leased" out for service without financial compensation. Countless men and women were "forced to work for free" for the duration of their unfair and exaggerated jail sentences, causing them "re-enslavement." Who knows how long these sentences were imposed on these people! Andrew Johnson came into power in 1865, so this practice went on for nearly 80 years and well into the Presidency of Franklin Roosevelt, ending in 1942. So essentially, slavery ended in America sometime in 1942 (RSWS: 1, 4, 5, & 6).

I will note at this point that although the Native peoples were stripped of their Nations and lands, then segregated, corralled, and cruelly treated, they have recently received some reparation in the form of casinos, which, in my opinion, still fall atrociously short of being considered adequate compensation for their sufferings, loss of dignity, land, and life. From my learning of their populations at the time of the colonial invasion, they were estimated to be between 12 and 15 million. After they were moved and resettled onto designated "Reservations," today, their population is less than 1 million.

I call that an eradication and extermination! We rightfully keep fresh in our memories that over 6 million Jews were eradicated/exterminated in Nazi Germany during World War II. Think about this, over 6 million Jews, 12 to 15 million Indigenous People, and at least 250 million of my enchained ancestors from Alkebulan died during the "Middle Passage" alone.

Also of note, the Japanese-Americans who were put in internment camps during WWII were finally compensated several decades later with reparations. And although it was said to have been promised to the formerly enslaved that they would receive "40 acres and a mule" as some part of reparations, with few exceptions, it never came to fruition, nor was anything ever granted to them or to us, to this very day!

As I've repeatedly written, I'm very sympathetic to the plight of the Native American population; however, I would be remiss in my duty of disseminating factual information if I didn't mention the fact that Native Americans also enslaved some of the people of my heritage.

To the contrary, after the Reconstruction period was abruptly squelched and ended, what quickly followed was a series of enacted laws, statutes, and court cases that disenfranchised and nullified most of the little progress that was made economically, educationally, and politically for the formerly enslaved, leading to today's inequities (RSWS: 1, 2, 4, 5 & 6). When I say leading to today's inequities, I mean it's still ongoing. So again, I ask, when did the mistreatment and unfair practices against the people who share my heritage ever stop? The unfair practices that began at "Emancipation" continuously morphed through to today with no end in sight!

"Make America Great Again." Very few people of my heritage, past or present, would or could say that America has lived up to her "full Greatness." Only those who still revere Andrew Johnson would! Again, you can't show me the period of American history that she's been fair, let alone great, to all her people and particularly to those of my heritage.

It's still yet to come! At best, we can only "MABA" or "Make America Better Again." I reiterate that whenever the country makes a stride towards progress, there inevitably comes a series of digressive setbacks. It's always one step forward, then several steps backward. For example, you heard former president Skunk's latest version of MAGA, now "MAGAA" or "Make America

Great Again, Again." And he's serious! How many unnecessary steps backward will the country take before finally stepping up and stepping forward to make real and lasting progress? Currently, America looks as if it's stepping backward off a cliff.

(Well, What About Reparations?)

Do I feel reparations are still in order for the sufferings of the people who share my heritage in this our country of birth? YES, I DO! And, by extension, to my distant cousins on the Alkebulan continent as well. The sufferings of our people have been relentlessly continuous in all the phases of our lives, with new and inventive twists constantly emerging.

I had the opportunity to watch a video by Shawn Rochester, the CEO of Good Steward LLC, Financial (https://www.youtube.com/watch?v=0w3o8uHVkKQ), on the quantitative study on the cost of the enslavement of the forcibly imported people of my heritage. It was quite extensive and clear. I lost track of the video link until literally days ago, but before rediscovering it, I had come up with my own general reparations package, and the following is what I initially wrote:

What I'm about to propose FALLS FAR SHORT OF WHAT I THINK IS FAIR, JUSTIFIED OR RIGHTEOUS. I personally feel the numbers should be higher and I haven't worked out the financial details down to the penny. Also, I don't want to break the American economy either.

The following financial statement is a rough draft, and I feel that no less than half of the numbers reflected should be the "bare minimum" reparation: For every non-immigrant American-born person of my heritage alive and those unborn in their mother's womb, at the time of the "said agreement," should receive the tax-free reparation of $1 million. According to the 2020 census, the people of my heritage make up 12.6% of our population, or 41.1 million people. That would be a reparation of roughly 41.1 trillion dollars, with half that number being roughly 20.5 trillion dollars.

This part of the Reparation is based on the period of time beginning with the start of slavery (1619) to the commencement of the agreement (currently 2022 totaling 403 years and counting). So let me add my two cents: For the next 200 years, we should be free from paying tax on any and all purchases. Make all contracts standardized to include a 2% higher (Statewide and Federally guaranteed) interest rate on all interest-bearing accounts, stocks, bonds, CDs, IRAs, annuities and, treasury notes, etc; a 2% lower than federally listed finance rate on all long-term purchases like real estate, transportation vehicles and business loans, etc… This would present an opportunity for us to recover some of the massive stolen and lost generational wealth swindled from the people of my heritage since the Reconstruction Era.

While searching for Mr. Rochester's lost video, I revisited Google and typed in, The video on the quantitative study done on the cost of slavery as it relates to reparations." Although I couldn't locate the actual video at the time, most of the listed articles didn't come close to my "guesstimated" thoughts on the cost of our receiving reparations. One article stated a 10-12 trillion dollar package. Another effectively stated we receive $800,000 per person, which I feel would be fair.

Another reason I say reparations are in order is if you look at the wealth income gap after all these years of "freedom" and having received no reparation from enslavement, segregation, and the underhanded dealings and setbacks due to the continuous "unlawful" civil acts and legislation being chronicled in and outside this book, that includes the "Black Codes," the over 25 some odd massacres and voting rights restrictions, etc… In America today, according to the 2020 census, the ethnic averaged median household income in US dollars listed: Asian=$94,908; White=$74,912; Hispanic of any race=$56,321; Native=$49,906; and Black=$45,870. The Asian population has more than doubled our income, and whites have roughly 66% more available to their households than those sharing my heritage.

Via: Google Search

U.S.; US Census Bureau: 2020

Source: US Census Bureau @ Statista 2021

(Drowned Towns!)

Additional reasons why reparations are in order is: I also recently learned a shocking fact that a surprisingly large number of cities, towns, and communities have literally been "washed off" the map and/or submerged under water under the guise of what is called "Development Induced Displacement" aka "DID." What they "DID" was invoke this form of eminent domain Public Works Community Development projects for the creation of lakes, parks, and other Public Works projects, affecting both black and white communities.

However, the disparity occurred in two ways. First, the vast majority of displaced communities were of the people sharing my heritage, and second, our communities weren't fairly compensated, if compensated at all. This little-known fact is another example of major losses of generational wealth. Why is this a little-known fact? I would answer it's because American history is being suppressed and not adequately, fairly, or properly taught and as a result, the vast majority of Americans are simply unaware of it.

In other words, the "literal burial" of the information worked!

Here are some facts: In Forsyth County Georgia, there once existed the community/town of Oscarville. In 1912, two teenage "black" youths were accused, tried, convicted, and sentenced, then executed all in the same day on a rape charge! Afterward, the white men in the area commenced to massacre an estimated 1,000 of its Black citizens. They then burned the community down. Soon after, they flooded the area, and today, it's called Lake Lanier. The town's still there, it just has water and perhaps boats floating over top of it these days. This was not the only community affected!

Also, there once existed a community called Kowaliga, Alabama. A couple highlighted features of the town were hosting a Black College and home to the first Black Railroad. Today, it's called Lake Martin. These types of projects weren't confined to the South either. In New York City, the "Black" community by the name of "York Hill" once existed. It was confiscated to build a "New Reservoir" to house a duck population. So, the "Ducks" were more important than the People! Most of the people from that community then moved into the nearby neighborhood of Seneca Village, which was also confiscated shortly thereafter, to create what is known today as the famous "Central Park."

It turns out that there are over 100 of these drowned-out towns and communities, aka "Drowned Towns," across America. The following is a short list of a few: Henry and McKee Islands, now under Lake Guntersville, Alabama. Vemport, Oregon, now called Delta Park. Other drowned towns and communities include Baird, CA; Elmore, CA; Kennett, CA; Morley, CA; Cebolla, CO; Dillon, CO; Sapinera, CO; Jerusalem, CONN; Old Fair, IN; Warren, MD; Dana, MASS; Enfield, MASS; Greenwich, MASS; Prentiss, MISS; Round Valley, NJ; Browns Station, NY; and Old Never Sink, NY to name a few of the over 100.

The Amber Ruffin Show:

Feb 12, 2022, on Peacock;

Segment: How Did We Get Here (Part 3):

Where are the missing Black Towns?

Because of the many men of my heritage who, since the institution of the "Black Codes," have been unjustly convicted, misrepresented, confronted with unfair racist jury selections and decisions and sentences of judges, as well as disproportionately incarcerated and later proven innocent (with most cases never being reviewed), I feel restitution/reparation is also in order.

I arrived at this conclusion because it, too, has shown itself to be rampant and unfairly systemic as well. I suggest that for every year, anyone (regardless of race or gender) who has been unfairly convicted should be paid reparation of whatever the average annual cost of incarceration was, tax-free and with compounded interest.

This type of disproportionate inequity is still prevalent today, as noted in our population to incarceration rates and averages. Statistics reveal that 1 out of every 3 "black" males will serve time in jail, whereas 1 out of 17 "white" males will be jailed. Also, the amount of time served for incarcerations are disproportionate as well.

While writing this book, I relearned on Chicago news that on October 20, 2014, police officer Jason Van Dyke was convicted of 2nd-degree murder for shooting 17-year-old Laquan McDonald 16 times in his back as he walked away from police armed only with a knife. 2nd-degree murder is charged when someone knows that the actions they are taking can result in the death. This "professional" police officer knew unloading his clip into the boy's back would result in his death.

Officer Van Dyke was sentenced to only 6 years and was released in February of 2022 after serving merely 3 years for "good behavior." I then learned that a person convicted of this charge served an average of 19 years if the victim was white. Via a Google search, I learned in the state of Pennsylvania, which is indicative of the entire country, when handing down life sentences, out of 100,000 cases, 53.1% went to people sharing my heritage, whereas only 2.5% went to whites.

In Laquan McDonald's case, I question the judge's decisions in the sentencing and the early release. It just doesn't seem fair, just or right. Other police officers implicated in the case never faced judgment. I argue officer Van Dyke was never in "fear" either, with so much police support surrounding him.

(Hatred Is Toxic)

In 2016, a term came to the forefront in American culture that was forever etched into our collective conscience. This most shocking term came to light as a result of the immigration policies enacted by former president Skunk at our Mexican border. What was disturbing to me is it took about 400 years before the term became recognized as an issue or problem because it had been practiced against the people sharing my heritage since America was stolen and colonized.

Former president Skunk alienated aliens, with most fleeing violent drug cartels and deadly regimes in several Central and South American countries as well as from Mexico. To rally support for his policies, using the media, his initial step was to raise the fear level among American citizens so his intended cruelty would seem justifiable by demonizing those seeking immigration, calling them criminals, gang-banging thugs, rapist, and drug dealers.

They were then corralled and crammed into tight living spaces that resemble facilities used for today's industrialized chicken farms. Do this sound familiar? At least they weren't "enchained" and corralled. Under his policy, border patrol personnel began separating children from their parents (most often their mothers). The problem was there was very little reuniting of parents with children, and frequently, the parents were sent back to their country of origin. As the broadcast news media learned of this forced separation of families and its effect on the children, the term that arose became known as "Toxic Stress."

The practice of fully separating children from their parents for the forcibly imported enslaved people of my heritage often began when they were initially enchained and even more so after they set foot on the shores of America and placed on auction blocks. That was if they survived the "Middle Passage" voyage! It was rare for an enslaved person to travel more than 10 mile from their plantation/imprisonment during their lifetime unless they were sold. Some never left the plantation during their entire lifetime. A parent could be sold to another plantation and forced to leave their children behind, or a child could be ripped from their parent's arms, then sold 15 miles down the road with them never seeing each other again. "Toxic Stress" was common to the enslaved.

A simple Google search on the topic reveals that Studies have shown associations between toxic stress and changes in the brain structure. The consequences of this can include more anxiety as well as impaired memory and mood control. Toxic stress responses can include changes in "gene expression," meaning which genes in your DNA are turned on or off. That's some serious scientific stressing!

(The Willie Lynch Letter)

Years ago, I viewed a DVD from my collection entitled "The Willie Lynch Chip." We live in this digital age where the pen is not often set to paper, but like programmed computer chips, it was felt the "slaves" could be controlled or "programmed" by a set of instructions or "codes" written in a letter on how to make the enslaved population docile in, accepting of and content with the conditions of enslavement.

Willie Lynch was a British slaveholder with a modest plantation in the West Indies (Jamaica). He was deemed an expert in the management of controlling slave populations. He guaranteed control through physical/psychological conditioning of the enslaved population that, if properly and robustly installed, promised its ongoing effectiveness for at least 300 years, even after being freed from enslavement.

He historically submitted his expertise in 1712 on the banks of the James River in Virginia at the request of American slaveholders experiencing insurrections (like the little-known, swept under the rug and largest insurrection of 1811 near New Orleans) and to keep their runaway enslaved populations in check.

He advocated taking into account and exploiting the differences in age, color/shade, fine or coarse hair, intelligence, sex/gender, and the general build of the enslaved. He also included additional classifying information such as the size, location, and State of the plantation, whether in a valley or on a hill, and regionally north, south, east, or west, all for the purpose of fostering divisions, distrust, and disunity amongst the enslaved. He intended them to trust only in the slaveholders and his white employee personnel (cronies), known as the overseer(s). (13) He promoted liberal use of the whip but not to the point of death and the loss of your investment.

He encouraged the enslaved to "tell on each other" or snitch for personal gain, a practice known as "Meritorious Manumission." This meant they would receive some form of reward, which, other than freedom, included being brought inside the house to work, eating leftover food from the slaveholder's table, day(s) off from normal laborious routines, or elevated to a minor overseer position and permitted to administer whippings to other enslaved deemed disrespectful, headstrong, unproductive or runaways.

Other divisive practices Willie Lynch encouraged was to have the light-skinned, who often were "Massuh's" or the Master's offspring, serve and sleep inside the house. They generally wore better clothing, ate a better quality of food, and generally were treated more humanely and lived more comfortably. They became known as the "house nigger" (aka the movie "Django"). They developed a tendency to flaunt their perceived status and were known to look down on the so-called "field nigger" whose mistreatment was noticeably harsher and regularly cajoled by the whip from the hand of the overseer(s).

Also of GREAT IMPORTANCE to note was the regular practice of the slaveholder to routinely rape and prostitute out our female ancestors for profit. This could cause further division within the family unit because she could be betrothed or married (with children), then contract an STD or get impregnated. As a result, the baby could be born obviously light-skinned, then go to work inside the household and develop some of those tendencies I just wrote about or not!

The child could live in the shack with the rest of the field hands with their mother, stepfather, and other family, which could possibly make for a very uncomfortable dynamic. A little-known fact is enslaved males were routinely raped, particularly by their female slaveholders, with some kept as concubines.

Truthfully, there is no actual traceable "The Willie Letter" to be found. After all, it wasn't a historical document written by the government like the Constitution. Somehow, a letter mysteriously appeared on the Internet in the 1990s, so its legitimacy has been questioned.

But because there were runaway slaves and many historically noted slave rebellions, the fact that the institution of slavery not only survived but thrived, flourished, maintained, and sustained for nearly 250 years before the Civil War arrested it, and since Willie Lynch did historically exist and traveled to the banks of the James River for the purpose of imparting his knowledge of a valid and well-document system of slave management to the American slaveholders on how to keep their enslaved populations docile, I consider the letter to have once existed.

Chapter: 3

FUNDAMENTAL FOUNDATIONAL FORMATIONS

(Some Earliest Memories)

Have you ever thought back to the earliest memories you can recall? If so, have any directly influenced your current perspective or life circumstances? After all, there is a saying that you live and learn. I've recently looked back and concluded some of mine have definitely influenced who I am today. With some, you might recognize a pattern. Others are a little more random and have little to do with who I am today.

The earliest memory I recall was a recurring bedtime one where it seemed I couldn't go to sleep until I heard my favorite song, "Green Onions," played on the radio or the "record player." I remember being in bed on my hands and knees, rocking back and forth until I heard it. The next thing remembered was waking up the next morning. I always felt my mother bought the record just for me after it fell out of rotation on the "WVON" radio station. I was at most 2 years old because I was born around Thanksgiving of 1960, and I learned the song was recorded in 1962.

A second memory was of my mother and Lucy, her closest friend, who was like an Aunt. They took me to the "show," what we called the movie theatre. I don't remember the movie, but after it ended, the screen rolled up, and lo and behold, a live band sat ready to play. I don't recall what genre of music they played, but in retrospect, I suspect it was Jazz. All I really remember was

Mother and Lucy stacking the coats and sitting me on top of them so I could better see. I was simply fascinated.

My stepfather had a role in my earliest memories. He nicknamed me "CB," meaning "Cry Baby." Later, it transitioned to "Little Buddy." Some Sunday mornings, he would take me with him to the Westside to visit his friend Curtis, who lived in the "Projects," so they could drink and listen to Jazz. Curtis' son constantly picked at me and forced me to wrestle with him.

Other times, he would take me with him to his childhood neighborhood on East 47th Street to listen to Jazz in the garage, where it cost $1 to go inside to sit and listen. However, most of the men stood in alley listening, drinking, and socializing, which was usually what he did. I have no doubt those memories are some of the reasons I've made my living in music as a performing artist and teacher.

Once my stepfather asked me to warm up some milk for a bottle, which had to be for my younger sister. He asked me to put a bowl on the stove and start heating it. So I got a bowl out of the cabinet, put it on the stove, and turned on the heat, only to see it start to melt. I remember traveling down to Tennessee with my mother and sister, my Aunt, and her 2 youngest boys in her car. I learned many years later it was for a funeral.

What I remembered was being in the kitchen watching my great aunt Josie baking a cake from scratch. She also made her own icing and glazes. I patiently sat there until she finished just so I could lick the residual batter off my fingers that was left in the bowl. It seems like she made a fresh cake everyday and she called me to the kitchen every time she did. I patiently sat right across from her, watching just so I could lick the bowl. Her cakes were so delicious, and I have a sweet tooth to this day.

Licking the bowl today wouldn't be permitted because of the raw eggs. However, I never got sick. Part of the reason I fell for my "baby's mama" was because she baked cakes from scratch. Over the last few years, I started baking my own cakes from boxed cake mixes.

I'll leave you with this one. I was sick with cold. It was difficult for me to sleep because I also had major chest congestion. I remember some kind of tea was brewed and that somebody suggested my mother put some whiskey in it with some extra sugar to help me drink it down and sleep. I slept like the "proverbial baby." When I woke the next day, I was "fit as a fiddle" and ready to "rip and run." Today, I'm not much of a drinker and have an herbal preference.

(The Twilight Zone)

An early memory that definitely shaped my current outlook and one of the reasons I wrote this book is my first recollection of race relations in America. I started kindergarten at age 4 because CPS policy at the time allowed for my early entry before the December 3 deadline. I didn't want to go to school, and I cried several days to the point that my stepfather nicknamed me "CB." My siblings made sure the nickname stuck with me for many years to come. Overall, I was a bashful and sensitive child.

It was the summer after 1st grade, and I was 6 years old when our family moved to 55th and Carpenter, where I learned of racism. As young children like to do during the summer, we got permission to go to the park, which was a short walk of 3 blocks west and one block north across Garfield Boulevard into Sherman Park at 54th and Racine. When I think back now, knowing what I know, it should have been named "Stonewall Jackson" Park because little did we know we were stepping into another dimension. Being so young and naïve, we didn't know this other dimension was known as "The Twilight Zone!" A place that was rife with strife, terror, and where unexpected danger lurked.

(Some People Don't Know Fear)

Do you know what fear is? Do you understand what fear can do to a person? I feel that some people don't know what "real" fear is. I'm not talking about being scared, like riding a roller coaster for the first time. I'm talking about the life-threatening, adrenaline-peaking, blood-curdling, racing pulmonary, the chest-pounding heart attack level mixed with total confusion and panicked type of FEAR!

If you understand that type of fear, I believe you're unlikely to cause someone to experience that level of emotional stress and trauma. Obviously, there's a difference of opinion because some people have intentionally and repeatedly caused needless fear to others. The human body can't sustain this "fight or flight" level of impending danger for very long without some type of breakdown, whether physically, emotionally, or both.

Fear is defined as an unpleasant emotion caused by the belief that someone or something is dangerous, likely to cause pain, a threat, or an often strong emotion caused by anticipation or awareness of danger. Some synonyms include fright, nervousness, sense of impending danger, panic or doom, terror, and threatening…I would add, causing bodily harm or death. It's not something we normally seek for ourselves. Professional daredevils might seek some level of controlled danger in a specific area of their expertise.

So there we were, these young, innocent, prepubescent, unassuming children without a single care in the world, fellowshipping with our new friends and simply enjoying all the amenities the park had to offer. We didn't know we were stepping into the "Twilight Zone." The "Outer Limits" of this Twilight Zone was Sherman Park. We weren't aware that north of the boulevard, the community was all white.

Sherman Park was idyllic, beautifully set with plenty of shade trees and a lagoon surrounding a small island that we named "Turtle Island" because you could find small turtles in the lagoon's water. We all wanted to explore the island but dared to go into the water because we couldn't swim, neither did we know how deep the water was. We eventually got to the island during the winter when the Lagoon water froze and later learned the water wasn't that deep either. It seemed to be a perfect summer day that wasn't too hot, with a gentle breeze blowing on our skin as we played on the slides, merry-go-round, in the sandbox, and "pumping" each other on the wooden bottom swings.

The etiquette of "pumping" each other could be a rather romantic gesture when it involved a girl pumping a boy because it led to her eventually sitting on his lap as they faced each other and because you usually didn't just pump anybody. But I digress. Suddenly, somebody in our group screamed RUN! This was because there was an angry mob of white teenagers and young adults racing toward us with sticks and bats, glass bottles and tin cans, and throwing bricks and rocks at us, screaming, "Git outta here niggers" along with other profanities! They were close enough for me to see the angry rage and hatred in their eyes and on their faces. I had never experienced anything like that before, and it was the first time I had heard the "N-word." This was the first time I (we) had to run for our lives, but it wasn't the last. And mind you, I was only 6 years old!

I remember it happened a few other times that summer. Once under the cover of darkness, the "mob" tried to sneak up on us. Another time, I was struck in the back by something. I don't know what it was and I didn't stop to check. Personally, the most frightening encounter occurred when I got separated from the group as we normally ran south on Racine Street, out of the park, and back across Garfield Boulevard.

This particular time, I panicked and ran east into their neighborhood, where some little boy around my age and size grabbed me, stopping me briefly, but not before etching something on my forehead with some chalk he had in hand. With my adrenaline racing and heart about to bust out of my rib cage, I shook him off and hauled ass to the end of the block and turned south, and ran through traffic back across the boulevard. When I caught up with everybody else, they asked me how did I get that cross on my forehead. In retrospect, I don't know if it was a Christian or KKK cross. Fear doesn't get more real than run for your life, somebody's trying to kill you for no reason at all!

The following November, I turned 7, and in early April of 1968, "Racism" was forever etched into my psyche. I wasn't aware of Rev Dr. Martin Luther King Jr until April 4, 1968, the day he was murdered in Memphis, Tennessee. The coverage was all over the news. It felt as if that was the first time I had watched the news. So many people were crying. I saw fear and worry in the eyes of the people who shared my heritage. I saw it in my mother. There was a sense of hopelessness rising amongst our people. I learned someone assassinated this man who only sought peace, equality, and fairness for all people in this country. I began to see that America simply had an evil streak in her underbelly.

While watching the network news later that day, I saw violence exploding all over the country. I saw fires burning in every major city. Violence didn't escape my neighborhood either. There was immediate resentment and backlash towards white people at that point. I was attending Oliver Wendell Holmes elementary school on 55th and Morgan, and although there were no properties burned down, I saw a white kid get beaten up in front of the school. A couple months later, while we were playing baseball on the boulevard, we witnessed one of my older brothers literally steal a white boy's bike. When the boy refused to voluntarily give up his bike, my brother cracked him over the head with a wooden stick from a broom or mop, breaking it in two and taking the bike.

I don't recall being chased out the park after that anymore. It seemed that almost overnight, the phenomenon known as "White Flight" had taken place. I also heard the "nigger" word over and over again that evening on the news. I was raised never to accept the word, and there was a saying in my area that when anybody called you a nigger, the reply was, "If I'm a nigger, you a trigger, suck my dick and make it bigger." I don't know where the vile saying originated, but after the park experiences and Dr. King's death, at that time, if you called me one, you could expect the saying to roll off my tongue like an automatic reflex.

After becoming acutely aware of the word, ironically, the only place I heard it after that was in my own community and sometimes on TV because Chicago was and still is a very segregated City for the most part. And although many in our communities have adopted and/or accepted it, the word, to this day, is not a part of my general vocabulary. It seems hypocritical to me to perpetuate such a foul word. However, I don't judge others for using it, but I will let you know that I'm personally offended by it if you call me the "N-word." But as the saying goes, to each, it's own.

It dawned on me that some people "DO" know fear, like God Bless them and their hearts, members of the military when having to go into battle. However, today, they sign up for service and go in with their eyes wide open, with full knowledge of the possibility that their life could be at stake. Police can experience a particular type of fear, and like the military, they sign up to serve. Although their jobs can be very dangerous, I feel what they most often experience is a level of anxiety, which is a fear of the unknown for a given set of circumstances. The Capitol Police in Washington DC definitely experienced fear on "Insurrection Day," January 6, 2021, when fighting to save American Democracy, as they were attacked with at least 140 of them severely beaten and several eventually losing their lives.

I also reflected on Dr. Martin Luther King's experience while marching here in Chicago, less than 2 mile down the very Street and Park that we, as little children, got chased out of. It was generally by the same people and personality types that he experienced exactly the same fear that we had.

Most of Dr. King's marches were peaceful and basically "civil." But if you listen to his recounts of marching in Chicago through the Gage Park neighborhood for fair housing, aka the "Jim Crow" of the North, you clearly hear the fear he had for his and all the other surrounding people's lives, as they peacefully marched through that neighborhood after being attacked. He stated it was worse than anything he had experienced in the South. In that instance, Dr King experience the same type of fear that I did in my childhood. Dr. King's march in Gage Park and the Insurrection at the Capitol was done by the same type of people. They haven't gone anywhere, if fact, they are well-represented today!

Chapter: 4

SEGREGATION GOOD... INTEGRATION BAD

(After Emancipation)

What actually happened after the Emancipation Proclamation? How the end of slavery led to the Holocaust-like starvation and death of 25% of the freed Black Americans at that time? Via a Google search, I found an article in the Guardian by Paul Harris, dated June 8, 2012, which goes on to say, "In the brutal chaos that followed the Civil war, life after emancipation was hard and often short." It reveals that hundreds of thousands of liberated slaves during and after the American Civil War died from disease and hunger.

An analysis done by historian Jim Downs of Connecticut College, casts a shadow over this most celebrated narrative of American history, which portrays the freeing of the slaves as a triumphant righting of wrongs that kept millions of Black Americans enchained on southern plantations. His book, "Sick From Freedom," illustrates the chaos of war most often fell brutally short of the positive image that has been portrayed. The newly freed were often neglected by Union soldiers or faced rampant disease that included outbreaks of smallpox and cholera. Many simply starved to death. His records reveals that it was believed that about a quarter of the 4 million freed slaves either died or suffered from illnesses between 1862-1870. That's about another million "Black Lives" lost. Did "All Lives Matter" in their situations?

He describes it as the largest biological crisis of the 19th century and the least investigated by contemporary historians. Downs states: "In the 19th century, people did not want to talk about it (and the country has never had a conversation about it)." Some did not care, and abolitionist, when they saw so many freed people dying, feared that it proved true of what some people said: "that slaves were not able to exist on their own."

His book also shares many stories about individual experiences of slave families embracing their freedom from brutal plantation life. However, many ended up in encampments called "contraband camps" near Union army bases, where conditions were unsanitary and food supplies were limited. Some contraband camps were also former slave pens. In many such cases, disease and hunger led to countless deaths.

What can you expect? Here, you are left to your own resources after coming out of enslavement with nothing nor given anything to help yourself, and you were expected to first survive, let alone thrive! Although the enslaved life was cruel and degrading, you were at least fed something to eat and drink. Imagine if those immigrants coming across our Southern border today are simply put in camps with no food, water, or any type of services provided to them. This would be considered cruel and inhumane.

Our ancestors experiencing those conditions were actually refugees within their own country of birth. If that type of unusual mistreatment were happening today, the news media would be all over it just as they rightfully were for president Skunk's policy of separating children from their parents was exposed. But that's what was done to these newly emancipated people. Again, I have to ask, "Did All Lives Matter," then?

(Some Things Don't Always Work Out As Intended)

(RSWS: 1, 2, 3, 4, 5, 6, 7, 8, & 9)

Upon further review, in many ways, segregation was good! I'm sure some eyes have popped wide open with that statement. Most people, at some point, have reflected back to some difficult period in their life. What caused this stressful time? Was it something you did or did not do, or was it caused from some outside force beyond your control? If you could go back and change it, would you? Why or why not? Or, if given the opportunity, would you do it all over again exactly as you had done before? The bottom line is, did you learn anything from it?

Honestly, "Segregation and Separate But Equal" weren't meant to be good things for the formerly enslaved. It was intended to put us out of sight and, therefore, out of mind and constructed by and for the existing power structure so they wouldn't have to think about or be bothered with the formerly enslaved people in any way, form, or fashion.

However, it didn't work out as intended, and they still had to contend with us, which once again manufactured something in their character that was very destructive and hideous, as with Tulsa, Oklahoma, in 1921 being only one example of that ugliness. And despite their intended subjugation, in many instances, we managed to manifest magnanimous monetary magnificence out of what was meant to be a momentous myriad of meaningful monetary madness and machination.

It was a tenuous triumph over torturous terror. I remember telling my buddies long before I wrote this that "They" established the first terrorist groups in America during the Reconstruction years with the Ku Klux Klan, aka the KKK, and as I've recently learned, along with "The White League." Over the intervening years, these terrorist groups have updated and expanded their base collectively called "White Nationalists." You can, with all the "pride" you can muster, specifically call one group "The Proud Boys," which reminds me of the "good 'ole boys." Can I get a yeehaw!

Other white nationalist and paramilitary-styled groups include the Minute Men, the Oath Keepers, The 3 percenters, and your everyday run-of-the-mill Neo-Nazis. And even worse, the "White Christian Nationalist." We were terrorized long before those groups existed by professional slave catchers who were also known to drag some non-enslaved people into enslavement. Today's "catchers" may be referred to as the police. Oh, by the way, recently, in some places, legislatively, the police were able to legally "stop and frisk" us at a whim (reminiscent of the "Black Codes").

Another longtime terrorizing practice in my community came to be known as "DWB" or "Driving While Black," where police are known to pull you over simply for being "black" and/or suspicious in their eyes. This happens most frequently if there are 2 or more people in a vehicle, especially males. They always seemed to be in search of any type of "contraband" or open alcohol within the vehicle that would give them the opportunity to make arrests.

You could be stopped for petty offenses like what happened to me once, for not making a complete stop at a stop sign. On this occasion, I was going to the CPS Teacher's Jazz Band rehearsal. I didn't know I was being followed because they were in a small, unmarked " Chevy Astro" van. When I made the so-called "California Roll," the lights came on, and out jumped 3 officers with their hands on their side firearms.

The police are "rarely wrong" and protected by governmental immunity. Although they've been known to lie after having been caught on video, in the vast majority of instances, they are subsequently freed to continue unleashing their "policing activities" on people like me. With the fewest of exceptions, the only police I ever see face consequences for bad behaviors are those sharing my heritage.

(Some Actual Pros And Cons Of Segregation)

I will dig into some pros and cons of segregation and the separate but equal doctrines. While acknowledging it WAS NOT intended to be a successful venture for the formerly enslaved population, the fact is, the legislation of the separate but equal doctrines were an all-out war against us and our successful integration into the fabric of American society. Have you heard the saying of, "a different day, the 'ole same S#!+." The point I'm making is that today looks eerily like the days of segregation and separate but equal, legislatively and as we know, that controls everything.

Our greater grandparents had to endure and overcome being cheated through the system of sharecropping. It was an institution specifically designed to systematically keep them financially enslaved. It took advantage of the government's lack of fulfilling a proper Reconstruction and/or any reparation assistance (RWSW: 1 & 2). Getting an education was "unofficially" highly discouraged.

Separate but "Unequal" manifested and officially penalized them with (Plessy v Ferguson). During that time, especially in the South, if white people knew you were "educated," you'd likely be deemed and called "a smart nigger." This often was justification enough for them sending their terrorist wing, the KKK, to burn you and your family out, perhaps kill you, often by lynching, or both.

With that, our ancestors were denied a fair and equally adequate education. This resulted in their financial suffocation. It severely stifled them from financing their own economic opportunities and growth. With this lack of education and inability to read and write, not only were they forced into the sharecropping deals where they "put their mark," which usually was an "X" on agreements they didn't fully understand, but nevertheless were made legally accountable for.

They were likely told one thing, which was a "big lie," then told they had consented by way of marking their X on the document. The fact was, they were most always duped and incurred debt as a result of these conniving verbal deals. For example, they incurred inflated costs of the grain or tools and equipment needed to farm the land. This financial entrapment was a means of keeping them enslaved and literally working the former slaveholders' lands for free. This was a direct result of their not being fairly and properly integrated and educated into American society and is just one example of how a systematic financial plot and application became systemic in the country for the next 100 years as part of an all-encompassing "Jim Crow" system.

To attempt to put a positive spin on their dreadful conditions, these sets of institutionalized laws of segregation and separate but equal did, at a minimum, afford our greater grandparents a meager opportunity to develop institutional parallels to that of white America. Because the people of my heritage were no longer permitted or allowed in white communities, at the very least, our communities had to have their own gas stations and grocery stores, hotels, nightclubs, hospitals, and attorney offices, as well as theaters, churches, and sports teams that often rivaled that of their white counterparts, despite the inherent setbacks.

Today, you don't see us having and owning our own businesses in our communities as it was during the segregation era. Therefore, our dollars don't circulate or matriculate within our communities, so, for example, we observe Arabs (we call them A-Rabs) controlling gas stations and the small, smelly grocery and liquor stores. Asian (Koreans) operates the ladies beauty supplies stores, and the people from India's heritage run the Baskin-Robbins franchises. You only see our people owning Barbershops and Beauty Salons, braiding, cutting, curling, and styling hair.

(Massacres: "Mass Acres," The Costly And Deadly Consequences Of The "Big Lies")

I stated earlier of my interest in breaking down words and discovering their root origins and twists that often reveal a deeper meaning. For example, I cited the word "nice" being an old French word taken for the city of "Nice." When I examined the word "massacre," basically, it means an indiscriminate and brutal slaughter of people. Also implying to unnecessarily murder large numbers of people. In the historical past, most massacres occurred as a result of War or because of religious differences. In America, massacres have primarily happened to the people of my heritage, and there is a recognizable pattern based on the spreading of a "Big Lie."

When I initially thought of a massacre in America, the only one that came to mind was the infamous "St Valentine's Day Massacre" in Chicago. For whatever greedy and selfish reasons, some "white" mobsters "rubbed out" or killed "a few" other mobsters. Al Capone's mob attempted to kill "Bugs" Moran, but due to time and chance, instead ended up killing several members of his mob. Some of the reasoning had to do with "turf" or the area where they conducted their illegal alcohol production and distribution activities during America's prohibition era. Today, drug dealers control certain "turf" in cities around the country.

More recently, I've learned there were more than 25 "lesser-known" massacres that happened to the formerly enslaved people sharing my heritage, that killed substantially more than just "a few" people, long before and after the St Valentine's Day event, that didn't get any of its notoriety or publicity. In fact, they were, as much as possible, swept under the rug and suppressed and, for the most part, forgotten and lost in the annals of "American History."

I will identify several of them shortly. Only one of the large number of murderous events has recently come to light, "The 1921 Tulsa, Oklahoma Massacre," aka "Black Wall Street." I purchased a DVD recounting the event somewhere around the turn of the Millennium and shared the information every chance I got.

When I break the word Massacres into two words, it becomes "Mass Acres," and unlike the one on Valentine's Day where "a few white criminal men" lost their lives, all the other massacres involved not only the loss of "innocent black lives," but mass amounts of acreage, where massive acres of land and lives and potential generational wealth were lost. It seems peculiar how they all involved the loss acres of people sharing my heritage and that they began immediately following the country's enslavement period, starting during the shortened "Reconstruction Era" and throughout the lawfully legislated institutionalized segregation decades.

It wasn't until the "Civil Rights" movement began and into the 1960s before TV network news began broadcasting these smaller-scale murders and other race-related atrocities committed by white citizens, municipalities, and police that some murders began to be recognized and acknowledged. Some have expressed it was because the movement drew in many fair-minded and upstanding Jewish and White Citizens.

A common thread running through most these "lesser known murders and massacres" was due to a "Big Lie" often told by a "white woman." Let us not forget there were untold numbers of individual murders that occurred to the men of my heritage due to this same type of "Big Lie." A prime example of this occurred to 14-year-old Emmett Till of Chicago while visiting in Mississippi.

The accusing woman, in her '80s, fairly recently confessed that she lied about young Emmett Till whistling at her before she died. Her "big lie" initiated a plot to first kidnap the innocent boy by several men from the community before they torturously murdered the poor boy before throwing him into a swamp. The plot was uncovered shortly after the murder took place. The "guilty" men were tried and found innocent by an all-white jury. One man later confessed he had participated in the murder but was never tried because of the "double jeopardy" law.

After Emmett Till's murder was reported, it got National and International attention, largely due to his mother's brave decision to have an open casket funeral service, where his badly beaten and bloated body was on public display for the world to bear witness to, which spurred the civil rights movement. We later learned the details of the lie and his subsequent murder, but the question remains, how many of these types of murders went unreported that have never come to light?

As with young Emmett Till, most often, the common trend of these "murders or massacres" was the reporting of the information was vague, with the number of murdered victims going under-reported and the guilty participants were rarely, if ever, brought to Justice.

Despite the variety of media I've acquired on these types of unsettling experiences in our American historical journey, I was aware of only 2 of the more than 25 of these loosely documented massacres, Tulsa, Oklahoma, and Rosewood, Florida. The "Rosewood Massacre" was turned into a movie. I will share information on several other of these mostly buried incidents, starting with Tulsa, and provide the limited details surrounding it, then list the skeletal information on 9 others in chronological order. Although the information can be found in other published materials, a Google search reveals much.

Tulsa, Oklahoma:

Of the many little-known massacres that happened to the formerly forcibly enslaved people of my heritage, the most well-known was the one that occurred in Tulsa, Oklahoma, known as "Black Wall Street." So named due to the affluent levels of achievement attained by that self-made community. Tulsa was indicative of the other less documented massacres.

This Tulsa community of great possibilities, prosperity, and hope was built by and for Black people, having places to work and live, learn, shop, play, and worship, was totally ravaged by the flames of a "hate-filled white mob" just over a century ago in late May 1921. The prosperous "Black neighborhood" comprising some 35-40 blocks was completely destroyed at the hands of this mob, killing hundreds of residents and burned down more than 1,250 homes, businesses, churches, and schools and erased decades of the people's hard work, ingenuity, financial successes and incalculable lost generational wealth.

The neighborhood of Greenwood was a fully realized "Separate but Equal" antidote to the racial oppression of the time. Built around the turn of the 20th century in a Northern pocket of the city. It was a thriving community of commerce and family residential life to roughly 10,000 residents with Greenwood Avenue being the center and pulse of the Black business community.

Brick and wood-framed houses dotted the landscape, along with blocks lined with churches, grocery stores, gas stations and hotels, nightclubs, billiard halls, and theaters, with doctor, dentist, and law offices, thus earning the name of "Black Wall Street." What took decades to build was erased in less than 24 hours by racial violence, sending the dead into mass graves and forever altering family legacies by a furious and heavily armed "White mob" of looters and arsonists.

The initiating incident occurred on the morning of May 30, 1921. A young black man named Dick Rowland entered the elevator at the Drexel Building at 3rd and Main with a white woman named Sarah Page. The exact details of what followed are scant and differ somewhat. As a story goes, he tripped and stumbled into a "manually operated" elevator (meaning a person operated it by hand and was not always perfect in lining the elevator with the level floor to step in or out of. He was said to somehow touched the women while trying to prevent himself from falling.

The Tulsa police arrested Rowland the following day to investigate further, which eventually led to the confrontation between Black and White armed mobs, with Rowland being barricaded in the courthouse for his protection. Another, and most likely the primary factor driving the violence, was resentment toward the "Black" prosperity found in block after block in Greenwood, starting with the marquee block at 100th and Greenwood Avenue. In that single block alone, there were 4 hotels, 2 newspapers, 8 doctors offices, 7 barbers, 9 restaurants, and a half-dozen professional offices of real estate agents, dentists, and lawyers, along with a cabaret and cigar shop, all housed in one, two and three-story red brick buildings.

"The financial toll was evident in the 1.8 million in property loss claims filed at the time, which is 27 million today, as detailed in the 2001 State commission report. However, if we base it on the average cost of a house today, of which I will reveal shortly, that number becomes: $468,625,000 or Four hundred sixty eight million, six hundred and twenty five thousand dollars.

A fact that should be emphasized is many people couldn't or didn't file claims because they were murdered, with many other survivors simply leaving the city. Tulsa reported the loss of blacks lives at 36. However, a recent and more thorough report discovered that approximately 300 people were found in one single mass grave alone.

Those 35-40 blocks were first looted then burned to the ground. The comprehensive report revealed that this was one of the worst racial domestic terror attacks in the nation's history, along with the government's culpability. Some of the mob participants were government agents and the Oklahoma National Guard, who were called in by civic officials. None of these criminal acts were ever prosecuted or punished by the government at any level. Also lost to this account is the staggering loss of what could have been enormous generational wealth, possibly securing fortunes for their children and descendants. Had they been allowed to carry on that legacy, there's no telling where they (we) could/would be today.

By: Yuliya Parshina-Kottas, Audra D.S. Burch, Troy Griggs, Mika Grondahl, Lingdong Huang, Tim Wallace, Jeremy White, and Josh Williams Published in the New York Times, May 24, 2021

The fact is, the massacre extended up to the Presidency itself. Woodrow Wilson was president at the time. He was known as the first "Progressive Democrat," for whom "Black People," for the first time, tried voting outside of the Republican Party, aka the "Party of Lincoln." Were you aware that this heralded so-called "American Hero" permitted the first and only time America has ever dropped bombs on its own citizens! Dynamite (nitroglycerin) was dropped from planes during the Tulsa Massacre, reportedly killing around 70 people. Wilson also instituted segregation policies in Washington DC's Federal buildings, including the "White House."

Wilson also permitted and viewed the screening of the highly controversial movie "Birth of a Nation" inside the White House. The movie depicted Black men as raving mad, violently unrestrained criminals, murderers, and rapists of white women. The film used white actors dressed in "black face" makeup.

The movie created panic within the white community and spurred a major resurgence of the KKK, who then came out the closet and openly shamelessly paraded themselves in Washington DC, and in other places around the country. It should be noted that Woodrow Wilson was born a southerner from the state of Virginia! Is there any surprise he acted as he did? If he's considered an American hero, who then would be an enemy?

Colfax, Louisiana Massacre:

Easter-Sunday April 13, 1873. 7 years after the Civil War during Reconstruction, in a Parrish where blacks outnumbered whites. Approximately 150 African-American militia and 3 white members of the "White League," a supremacist organization similar to the Ku Klux Klan, were killed when whites stormed the courthouse after white Democrats spread rumors (a Big Lie) that the black militia planned to kill all the white men in the Parrish and ravage the white women to create a "new race." The White League announced "safe passage" to any Blacks wanting to leave town peacefully but reneged instead. The League began shooting and killing the unarmed blacks, then the militia.

They torched the courthouse, and those attempting to escape were shot and butchered, with their bodies thrown in the Red River and into mass graves. Several dead bodies were left to rot in public outside the courthouse as excavated bones revealed in the mid-20th century. The US Supreme Court case United States v Cruikshank (1876), levied against 4 of white participants, was thrown out and sent to the State Supreme Court, claiming it was a State issue. The state of Louisiana then refused to try the case at all.

Wilmington, NC Massacre of 1898:

Where Black and White elected officials shared power. In this instance, a white women erroneously reported that she was "threatened" by black men. The white men of the town made a "declaration of independence" and went on a rampage, overthrowing the entire city government, killing (black) people, and destroying significant parts of Wilmington's properties, including their printing press. It was reported that 60-300 Blacks were killed in this act of domestic terrorism. It was covered up until year 2000.

Atlanta, GA Massacre of 1906:

An unfounded accusation alleged that some black men raped 4 white women. Some 2,000 white male terrorists began the slaughter by beating, stabbing, and shooting a disabled man, then went on to kill an unofficial death toll of some 100 blacks.

Elaine, Arkansas Massacre of 1919:

This incident is known as the deadliest confrontation in Arkansas history and possibly the bloodiest in America. Black citizens outnumbered the white population 10 to 1. The Black Sharecroppers, recognizing they were forced into a perpetual financial deficit, were seeking economic justice and sought to form a union. When they held their meeting, it was rioted by the Whites.

Initially, one white man was shot and killed, then hundreds of white men attacked what they called the "insurrection," killing an estimated 200 black people, including women and children. Some were arrested and tortured while in custody. 12 black men got the death penalty. When the case went to court, the NAACP represented them (US v Elaine 12) and got them freed.

Interestingly, they called it an insurrection, whereas so many people today refused to call the 1/6/21 attack on our National Capitol and governmental infrastructure anything less. To be noted: The race riot in Chicago occurred in the summer of that year.

Rosewood, Florida Massacre of 1923:

Like the Tulsa Massacre, the community was burned to the ground. A white woman (Fanny Taylor) claimed being assaulted by Sam Carter, a blacksmith who was the first man killed. After being tortured and mutilated, his lynched body was hung from a tree. 150 black people were reported killed, with many escaping by hiding in the nearby swamps for days. There was a Grand Jury convened that decided there was not enough evidence available to prosecute the case. A movie was made of this historical event.

Incident at Columbia, TN 1946:

This particular February 25 & 26 incident involved military veterans unwilling to accept the racial norms after returning to their hometown after serving in WWII. Strained race relations in the town from a 1925 lynching had eased up somewhat until Feb 25, 1946, when James Stephenson, a US Naval veteran, accompanied his mother to pick up her repaired radio. The young white male clerk got into an argument about the repaired bill with James' mother. James stepped between the two after the argument became heated. The clerk, who had threatened James' mother, was thrown and crashed through the window during the struggle.

The police arrested James and his mother on a disturbing the peace charge, for which they paid the $50 fine and were released until later that day when James was arrested again because the clerk's father filed a felony warrant charge of assault with the intent to kill. Locals posted his bond.

That night, a white mob gathered around the Maury County courthouse, a block south in the segregated black business district of Mink Slide, where blacks and military veterans had gathered. The police chief sent in 4 patrolmen, and someone shouted for them to stop. When they didn't, shots were fired, wounding a patrolman. Within hours, State Police and the safety commissioner arrived together with other whites and surrounded the Mink Slide district. The next morning, the State Police went in, firing shots into random buildings. They stole cash and goods and searched homes without warrants.

They confiscated some 300 weapons and arrested at least 100 people. None of the people were permitted to post bail or allowed legal representation. Thurgood Marshall, the future US Supreme Court Justice, and the "NAACP," came in when the situation intensified further after two prisoners were killed on February 28th. The incident also cited a threat to the life of Mr. Marshall, as he and his team were leaving the area when State patrolmen harassed and stopped him and eventually arrested him with an accusation of drunk driving. Rather than taking him to the police station, the patrolmen drove him into a rural area off the road. However, a white assistant of Marshall's followed them the entire way, which thwarted their suspected attempt to lynch him.

Chapter: 5

FEEL AS IF ANYTHING IS POSSIBLE, THEN...

I was born in the 1960s. I call it the decade of hell and hope. Why? I shared with you the story of one of my earliest memories of being chased out of Sherman Park at 6 years old by a violent white mob that forever shaped my consciousness, then months later, at age 7, learning of the deaths of Dr. Martin Luther King and several other civil rights leaders. Those were terrifying and tumultuous times in my life. By contrast, the Civil Rights Movement was reversing instituted segregation laws, then putting men on the moon and safely returning them in 1969 was revolutionary and gendered a hopefulness that, in my opinion, pushed into the 1970s and the early1980s.

I felt that good things were happening. It seemed America was actually living up to her Creed, promises, and proclamations by finally correcting herself and healing the ills she had inflicted upon the people she previously withheld the promises of Life, Liberty, and Justice, and the American Dream from.

America was now "affirming" herself by demonstrating through "acts" of fairness and equity previously denied to the people she had formally and informally enslaved legally by law and later through legislation and lynching and her lustful, lecherous, lascivious behaviors. The country was finally balancing the scales for the people it had denied life, liberty, and justice with "Affirmative Actions."

I enjoy and often imitate the dialects of people all around the world. I find it fascinating how a word pronounced by our white population might be sounded differently in the communities of my heritage. Remember, part of the reason for this is that our people had and have continuously been denied equal educational facility mixed with our natural ancestral dialects.

One such word is "renege." Amongst the white population, the "neg" part of the word sounds out as in the words "negative" or "egg," whereas in my community, it most often sounds out as "nig" as in the words "trigonometry" or "trigger." Well, it turned out that the white population once again reneged on the promises we felt would come to pass as a result of the Civil Rights struggles and legislation, so they became "renegers." In my community it would most likely sound out as "reniggers."

The term "Affirmative Action" morphed into the "Reverse Discrimination" joke! Today, some people pretend things have always been fair or "equally discriminatory." They would argue there has never been any discrimination in this country. I say prove it and start the race at 1619 like I'm doing!

You'd be a cheater because you've had a head start of about 350 years by 1970. How can you expect "me" to compete, let alone win a race, with you having such a vaunted lead? It would be as if we were racing the 100-meter dash, with me starting at the starting line and you starting at the 80-meter mark. America once again "reaffirmed" herself to be a liar.

(Change The Game In The Game)

A person could write several books, if not volumes, on how America has contradicted herself when it comes to what is written in the "Constitution" and what is or has been actualized in truth, especially as it relates to her formerly enslaved and Native inhabitants. Here, I will draw a very broad and abbreviated accounting of her falsehoods, as written in word, as opposed to the truthful acts that so often have been covered up, purposefully changed, submerged, and/or watered down and whitewashed.

To this day, America has refused to look herself in the mirror and accept how ugly she is and how foul she smells while proclaiming to be the "Shining light on a hill." This contradiction is a driving force as to why some people don't want our history fully and accurately taught. It's because of their personal guilty conscience, in that their hearts are in the same place as so many of the original conquering settlers of 1619, which demonstrates a lack of personal evolution that's fomented and taught generationally in family households, then by extension, nationwide.

To briefly review a few ways America has continuously "changed the game in the game" and repeatedly reneged, started at the founding of the country with the "enlightened Founding Flounderers," I mean "Founding Fathers" in how they generally denied rights to most "white" men and women, all the Native indigenous people, as well as to all the forcibly imported people of Alkebulan heritage, whom they enslaved and concocted the three-fifths compromise for.

Whereas they lied and wrote that "All Men Are Created Equal." When in truth, the requirement was simply to be a wealthy landowning white man. It shouldn't be forgotten that many "free" people of my heritage living in the North and others who actually migrated to America were often abducted and also forced into the tyranny of American enslavement.

After roughly 90 more year and the "Emancipation" of the enslaved, during the "Reconstruction Period," the 13th, 14[th,] and 15th Amendments were quickly reneged on, as the "Northern Repunkican" legislative governing bodies decided in another "Compromise of 1877" along with the former slaveholding "Southern Dimasscraps," to withdraw all the remaining peacekeeping troops from the last 3 southern states that abruptly end this brief period of reconciliation and reciprocity, so as "not to offend the Southern Insurrectionists" and further deny "them" of their "financial sustenance."

They then began to systematically deny the "formerly enslaved" proper educational and financial opportunity by legislating and constructing various financial schemes, including sharecropping and the denial of an equal or adequate educational opportunity, which allowed for the swindling of the newly emancipated people out of their duly proper financial opportunities and gains.

It was all reinforced by permitting the first terrorist organizations, like the "White League" and the Ku Klux Klan, to simply manifest themselves and exist to this very day as "White Nationalist" groups and Neo-Nazis, for example. Since the financial and educational opportunities to the formerly enslaved were formally "Deconstructed," this allowed for the "Reconstruction" of the racism that exists to this very day and demonstrates a clear example of how a systematic plot was hatched to begin what is now deeply embedded and systemic in our nation today!

I also find it very interesting how, during the enslavement period, the white (Southern) population insisted the "Black" slaves be all around them, in their communities, inside their homes, cooking, cleaning, and even rearing their children. Then, upon Emancipation, the formerly enslaved people of my heritage were banned from being anywhere around "these upstanding white people," mandating separation and distance. Blatant hypocrisy!

(Segration Registration)

So they introduced "The Black Codes," then "Segregation" and the "Separate but Equal" lies and doctrines to further deny equal opportunity and access to economic, educational, and political fairness, justice, equity, or equality (RSWS: 1, 2, 4, 5, & 6). Even after separating and kicking the formerly enslaved to the curb and into their own communities, when they managed to manifest any type of financial prosperity, white folk would then conjure up ways to dilute or eliminate that wealth with, for example, "eminent domain Public Works projects," or even worse, create the notoriously famous "Big Lie" and produce excuses to burn their entire communities to he ground in "massacres," causing yet to be totaled loss of life and loss of generational financial resources and wealth (RSWS: 9).

I call it "Segregation Registration." Separate but Equal was purposefully legislated and became the "Law of the Land." We realize it was "Separate but Un-equal!" The formerly enslaved were regulated to substandard everything but often still changed shit into sugar. But there has always been a powerful minority group of "haters" who always seems to get their way, just like today.

Another way this remnant group got their way was to use the separate but equal doctrine to "Red Line" sections of cities and towns. This permitted them to initiate funding irregularities and separate those formerly enslaved, who where once endeared to their homes and properties, to substandard, underfunded, and underdeveloped housing communities and neighborhoods. As a result, the property values became and are still the lowest in the country. Government and Corporate funding for development in these communities have been and remain at all-time lows.

Another atrocity occurred during President Franklin D. Roosevelt's signing of "The Servicemen Readjustment Act," aka " The GI Bill," into law on June 22, 1944. It was INTENDED to be managed by the Federal government, but during its drafting, it was successfully lobbied and undercut by Mississippi segregationist and Democratic congressman and Chairman of the House Veterans Committee, John E. Rankin, to have it managed at the local/city level. The GI Bill was intended to provide sweeping benefits for "all Veterans" that included fully paid college tuition, low-cost home loans, and unemployment insurance.

Recognizing the bill represented significant gains for Black Southerners, Rankin refused to cast the critical proxy vote in protest, thereby ensuring Black Veterans experience discrimination in application for, then being denied equity to the disbursement of funding, therefore having difficulty accessing its benefits for college and vocational training programs and to higher paying jobs, low-cost home loans and being able to live in integrated communities, as well as getting access to unemployment insurance as readily as White Veterans could.

The Federal government was again used via the United States Postal Service (USPS), who often retained the pertinent information at the post offices rather than deliver mail to the formerly enlisted military people of our communities to whom it was addressed. Rankin's systematic plot is another piece of what became systemic actions in denying Blacks access to wealth accumulation in both the South and the North, which was not free of its own discriminatory practices.

When President Eisenhower initiated his Nationwide Interstate infrastructure program, here again, State and City governments chose to "Redline" areas that most often ran through usually the most prosperous areas of "communities of color" and again separated the people from their wealth. Neither did these local governments provided fair, equal, or adequate financial compensation for their properties. In these instances, they used the label of "Eminent Domain." There always seems to be some imaginative twist when it comes to this country's deprivation to the people of my heritage.

For example, according to the Washington Post article by Erin Blakemore on August 17, 2021, titled "Interstate highways were touted as modern marvels. Racial injustice was part of the plan." The article states, "In cities, hundreds of thousands of homes had to give way for President Dwight D. Eisenhower's dream. 'A majority were in communities of color.' ...Take Interstate 77, which was greeted with fanfare in Charlotte. 'It'll be wide, handsome, and toll-free,' a 1959 newspaper gushed...In Charlotte, it meant bulldozing Brooklyn, a vibrant Black neighborhood where, former resident Barbara C. Steele recalled in a 2004 oral history, 'everybody knew everybody, and everybody was somebody.'... This type of displacement was more norm than (the) exception. Between 1957 and 1977, the US Transportation Department, more than 475,000 households were forced out for the highways' construction. A majority of those lived in urban communities with low incomes and high concentrations of people of color. ...."

To put this in the perspective of dollars and cents (common sense), mathematics will illustrate and illuminate the issue clearly. When I started buying the house I lived in for over 21 years, it was selling for $90,000. There was some refinancing, but after I had to relinquish the property, it was on the market for $339,000 dollars, a difference of $240,000 or roughly a quarter million dollars. Using $250,000 as the average cost of a house nationwide, then multiplied by the 475,000 households lost as previously indicated, this comes out to a grand total of $118,750,000,000 lost.

These numbers are so large that I will spell them out. One hundred and eighteen billion, seven hundred and fifty million dollars is the equivalent of potential accumulated lost wealth. If I knock off 75,000 homes on the account of affected white households, it still totals $100 billion dollars. The "actual" median cost of a house in the United States today is $374,900 x 400,000 households=$149,960,000,000 (One hundred and forty-nine billion, nine hundred sixty-million dollars) of accumulated wealth and/or potential lost wealth. These are staggering financial figures!

The Los Angeles Times reported, "Highway planners in Birmingham, Alabama, did the same thing when routing Interstate 59. ...After Ku Klux Klan leaders and others destroyed the Greenwood neighborhood of Tulsa, Oklahoma, a century ago in the nation's deadliest race massacre, residents quickly rebuilt the commercial area renowned as "Black Wall Street." But, the neighborhood was demolished for good when Interstate 244 and US 75 were built through its center in 1971. ..." On a personal note, in my observation of the highway system in my own city of Chicago, the claims previously stated holds true here as well. I will illuminate this claim, so please bear with me again.

Interstates I-90 and I-94 cross the country in an East-West direction, generally north of Chicago. However, both interstates move south into the Chicago area to go around Lake Michigan. While running through Chicago, I-90 runs in an East-West direction, and I-94 runs in a North-South direction. They combine in the downtown area and run south, eventually out of Chicago, before they separate again.

I live on the southern end of Chicago where I-90/94 continues but splits at 95th & State Street in its Southern direction, running on the Eastern end of the city as it exists Chicago leading into Indiana, where they split again, and I-94 goes north into Michigan, and I-90 continues on to all points east. Back at 95th & State Street is where I-57 begins and runs on the Western part of the city as it begins to exist Chicago, going south through Illinois. Both expressways cut through communities of people who share my heritage, and in between the two expressways are also the communities of people who are of my heritage. With circumstances being what they are, my family's home is near the first exit of I-57.

Returning back to from 95th & State and proceeding north on I-90/94, aka "The Dan Ryan," from 95th down to 63rd Street were historically white communities. 63rd North, down around to 22nd, which included historic "Bronzeville," was and still are the communities of people sharing my heritage. At that point, for about a mile or so to the west of the expressway, you have the Bridgeport community that historically has been one the most racist white communities in Chicago and host to the Chicago White Sox baseball team/ballpark.

Opposite that community on the East side of the expressway moving northward towards "Downtown," again to around 22nd, were still communities of my heritage that are currently undergoing "gentrification," a process known to displace the current long-standing population with overpriced housing that's usually unaffordable to most of them.

Back to the West side of the expressway, and after passing north through Bridgeport, you come into the area known as "Chinatown." Right around there, the expressway curves west and elevates for about 10 blocks before settling back down as it approaches the downtown area, where I-94 splits, continuing northward and to I-290, which takes you to the medical district and through the west-side communities of our heritage and eventually out of Chicago.

The two expressways have had that effect on our communities. While doing the math, I will calculate only the South branch of the highway's infrastructure through our communities and tally the massive loss of our properties and generational wealth because I grew up on the "south side" and am more familiar with the affected areas,

On I-90/94, aka the Dan Ryan, there are 41 blocks from 35th to 63rd and, like in my block, running east/west (facing north/south). There is an average of 30-32 houses/apartments per block. 41 blocks x 30 houses =1,230 units. The expressway also consumed an additional 41 blocks, averaging 40 houses totaling 1,640 homes running north/south (facing east/west). This figure now becomes 2,870 units. Monetarily, at today's average cost of a house and in the narrowest sense, the figure now becomes $974,350,650 (Nine hundred and seventy-four million, three hundred and fifty thousand, six hundred and fifty dollars) of wealth.

Again, this is not counting the West side expressway (I-90). This was regularly practiced in all the major cities across America. I can't account for the more rural areas. If I go back to Tulsa's Massacre and use today's average home matrix, the figures become $4,686,250,000 (Four billion, six hundred and eighty-six million, two hundred and fifty thousand dollars) as opposed to what was listed in the report of 2001 of 27 million. So, when I earlier originally calculated the reparation of 41.1 trillion dollars to the people of my heritage for today's reparation repayment, it begins to take shape.

By the way, I've Googled information on trying to find the number of Black contractors hired during the years initiating the interstate highway project with great difficulty, and as of this writing, I've had no success.

(You've Got To Be Over Qualified To Qualify)

In our community, there is a general consensus that to get the job, you have to be twice as good as your white counterpart. We already recognize that our credentials have to be sterling. Of course, this is not always the case. I reiterate that historically, we've been denied an equal education and have had to form our own Colleges and Universities of higher learning. Nevertheless, so often, we've heard ... "You're overqualified" after presenting our credentials.

Obviously, this is the LIE to deny! "Overqualified" means "I'm qualified" and then some. What's wrong with that? Just hire me in the position until another position comes along that allows for my extended qualifications. At the very least, I'm knowledgeable of the lower level inter-workings of the company, which should be an advantage for the company. The term "reverse discrimination" was also born out of this era as some white people claimed they were being denied employment due to the "quota system" or as an unfair apportionment. Simultaneously, the term "token Black" was introduced. This often meant you were the "only Black" minority to be seen in a company or firm.

(Come So Far, Yet Gone Nowhere)

Earlier I shared in a story of my first work experience after College in a local University's mailroom, where I met my closet friend Bobby. There was a third person working there, who also became a close friend and who was also born the same year as Bobby and me. Nat was born in April, Bobby in June and I was born in November of 1960. He also had his first child around the same time we did. When I started working there, Nat was a mail clerk, just as I was, but soon after was promoted to the second-level supervisory position, serving as the workforce/flow coordinator. He served only under the mailroom's director, Cleveland who we called Cleve. Everybody else served under them. Cleve was a couple years older than us and, like Bobby and me, was a College educated musician.

Both Nat and Cleve were white. Nat was one of those white brothers I considered to be open-minded, having a laid-back, hip sort of demeanor, and spoke from the streets, often using slang from the black community, or at least he attempted. He also lived in that most notoriously racist neighborhood of "Bridgeport," where former infamous Mayor Richard J. Daley and his son, former Mayor Richard M. Daley, both resided and raised their families. If you were a person of my heritage, you could safely venture as far as the Ball Park, which was conveniently located steps away from the Dan Ryan expressway's "Red-line L train" stop at 35th Street, which is part of the city's public transportation system.

Although Cleve was a musician, by contrast, he acted as if he had a stick up his butt. Personally, I believed part of his attitude resulted from my being a member of a band that got a record deal and whose music was playing on radio stations in Chicago, around most of the country, and in various parts of the world, that also charted in Billboard's top 100.

My friendship with Nat grew to the point that he invited me to his home several times to have something to eat with his family before going to the local indoor basketball gym to shoot hoops with his neighborhood buddies. Perhaps I was naïve or foolish to some extent, but I never felt intimidated or fearful when we fellowshipped, all the while knowing what that neighborhood was known for. People of my heritage were literally beaten and killed in Bridgeport.

At this chronological point in time, we had moved into the late 1980s. Bobby never cultivated the relationship with Nat that I had. However, it was about this time that the blinders came off my eyes, never to return. Nat had gotten demoted in his job functions back to a regular mail clerk. Cleve then elevated Ben, another young white guy around our age and a recent full-time hire, who had initially worked part-time in Mailing Service as a part of his "work-study" program to assist in paying off his college debt.

He generally was cool, too, but I think it was because he was around "educated black men" who pulled no punches. However, had I not known him, I wouldn't have wanted to meet him with his boys in Bridgeport, although he wasn't from that neighborhood. Nat was pretty closed mouth about his demotion, but it came down through the "grapevine" that it was because of a certain "fraudulent activity." During his tenure supervising, he never acknowledged being sick or going on vacation, so his sick time and vacation days never reduced, just increased, which meant when it came time to retire, all this additional time would become additional money towards his retirement package.

This information was actually confirmed by Ben, the new "minor" supervisor. None of us "brothers" openly made a big deal of it, but when the 5 of us privately talked, we agreed that had that been one of us, not only would we had been fired, but likely prosecuted and jailed. There were 3 kickers to this story. First, 4 of "us" 5 brothers working in Mailing Services had a minimum college education of an Associates Degree.

As I previously stated, the two of us having BA Degrees in Music, and one of us having 2 Degrees (Political Science and Computer Science), were never considered to fill the position Nat was demoted from, and Ben, a student at the University and relatively new full-time hire received.

The second kicker was, about 18 months later, Ben earned his degree and got hired as a State Police officer. You might guess where the story is going. Yes, Cleve re-promoted Nat back the same position he was demoted from. The final kick to the throat was learning Nat didn't have a high school education, not even a GED! He was cool with me and all, but the running joke became he had a "Jethro Bodine" education, a character from the sitcom "The Beverly Hillbillies," who boasted of his brilliance because he had a 6th-grade education.

This was beyond appalling to all of us. A couple years later, Bobby and I earned our K-12 Illinois Teacher's Certification and were out of there. I never hated on Nat, just the "system" that allowed for that. Naturally, becoming a teacher and no longer working in Mailing Services cooled my relationship with Nat. We were still friendly when I went back to visited the guys on school holidays or over the summer vacation from time to time.

That incident was the re-awaking of my feelings that, as a people of Alkebulan heritage in this country, that we as a people have "come so far, yet gone nowhere." It caused me to reflect back on some of the stories my mother shared with me of her frustrations working at Sears and working her way up from customer service to accounts receivable, then having to train high school graduates in her job only to see them promoted above her and becoming her supervisor(s).

(Sickness In Our Symbols)

I clearly began to see the irony of new twists on the same old game. The finding of ways to keep our families torn asunder, primarily through joblessness, the senseless killings by police of our men (and increasingly our women), and through exaggerated incarceration rates for petty crimes with graduated jail sentencing practices, etc…As I've heard it said by many in our communities, "It's the same 'ole same 'ole" or "A different day, the same 'ole shit!"

Yes, many of us have experienced success mostly via athletics, the clergy, and entertainment (RSWS: 3 & 7), but per capita, throughout all the venues of industry, it's far too little opportunity, equity, and justice. Overall, it feels dangerously daunting and depressing. This also led me to see the hypocrisy and sickness in our symbols.

Unfortunately, this is the reason so many simply give up or turn to crime or drugs that, then perpetuate these recurring cycles and ingrain them into the American psyche. "The Great American Dream," for us generally has been "The Great American Nightmare" and definitely "The Great American Lie."

Crimes have constantly and consistently been committed against us, forcing us to bare the blame and its shame. How can you "pick yourself up by your bootstraps" when you've never had booths in the first place? And, if you do manage to get a pair, so often they're ripped off your feet, like in Tulsa, Oklahoma. Again, the Indigenous people have their story to tell, but I'm speaking from my own learned experiences.

The sickness in our symbols is demonstrated by the words in the terms "E Pluribus Unum," or "Justice Is Blind," the "Blindfolded Lady Justice," and the words inscribed on the "Statue of Liberty" and in the "Pledge of Allegiance and the National Anthem." On the other end of the spectrum, you still have the Confederate flag being waved and pledged to with insurrectionists on January 6, 2021. That flag was only recently removed from the Mississippi State flag and finally taken down from flying in the State Capital of South Carolina.

The "Daughters of the Confederacy" took it upon themselves to have signs posted along the highways, particularly in southern towns, and had statutes erected under the guise of "Southern Heritage." We still have Civil War battle reenactments. Yet today, we still have significant numbers of influential people who only want selected pieces of American History taught and not the full story because of their personal tilt and guilt.

A debate has recently surfaced regarding Confederate statues and monuments continuing to be publicly displayed or be placed in historical museums. Many question whether they should've ever been erected in the first place. My question is, should the country erect statues to honor insurrectionist? If yes, then some will soon be erected to honor of the Jan 6, 2021 insurrectionists!

The issue came to my attention in 1978 upon attending Livingstone College in Salisbury, North Carolina. When I approached the small downtown area that extended one block north, south, east, and west of Innis & Main Street, there stood a statue of a fallen soldier being lifted up by angels, one on each arm. To summarize the lengthy inscription, it read: "This is in honor of all the soldiers who gallantly fought and died for the glory of the Confederacy…"

It's been a number of years since my last visit, but I wonder is it still standing, and if so, why are they still honoring insurrectionists? I remember wanting to bring it down at the time by any means possible! Teaching history doesn't mean teaching guilt. It's supposed to teach honest and truthful facts, whether favorable or not!

If you examine the conceptual lie of America being "the land of immigrants," as expressed by the words on the symbols of the Statue of Liberty (Which France commissioned, built, and donated to the United States as an acknowledgment that our country had broken the bonds and chains of slavery, and where the broken chains were supposed to be prominently displayed) and in E Pluribus Unum, they gloss over the fact that major groups of people didn't migrate to this land. Already here were the Native indigenous people, aka the so-called "Indians Nations," and Natives spilling over from the countries now called Mexico and Canada. Neither did my ancestors, the forcibly imported people of Akebulan heritage. Secondly, after all this time together, at this point, we've failed to achieve the "out of many, one" part of the equation.

When America began allowing large segments of (primarily white) immigrants into the country, they largely took jobs that were held by the people of my heritage. Sounds familiar? It could be called "The Great Replacement Theory." Today, America is one of the more segregated places on the planet, as exemplified by the general composition of our neighborhoods and attendance at Church on Sundays.

The government has made several attempts to legislate integration into our society with little success thus far. For example, the institutionalized doctrine of "Separate but Equal" should never have come into existence in the first place. However, in and of itself, it was never realized or properly instituted as an adjustment to the inequalities demonstratively imposed and manifested upon the people of my heritage.

It's always been "Separate but Un-equal" in every aspect of existence. I've barely mentioned and only scratched the surface on just a few of these inequities still affecting our daily lives and the dealings within our communities regarding Community Development projects, housing, jobs, and crimes and punishments (RSWS: 5 & 6).

A fairly recent practice and enactment of this dilemma is chronicled in the packaged labeling of drug use, with its imposed punishment, as we've learned through the news media. It was literally legislated then enforced by police and the judicial system. The fact is the people of my heritage, by and large, realistically, have never really had the financial means or connections to import illegal drugs into the country in mass. We've simply not had the money to do it! Money brings power. Power brings connections. Drugs are bought and brought in by a "white" frontman, who uses a "black" man as a middleman and distributor to their communities.

The law and media portrayed the "Crack epidemic," which primarily affected poor "Black" communities, as a blight or scourge on society in general, as well as a "crime" punishable by legislated laws. While at the same time, you had more "White" folk working on "Wall Street" and in other Financial districts around the country carrying and using cocaine on a daily basis in widespread use. But what happened to and against us was the creation of "Stop and Frisk" and "3 strikes you're out" legislation.

This edict came directly down through several Presidents, including Nixon through George Dummy Bush, enacted by State and local municipalities, then enforced by the policing community, accompanied by unfair and disproportionately lengthy sentencing and punishments imposed by the Judicial branches for often relatively small amounts of drugs. While at the same time, the "White guy" who had first purchased, then distributed, sold, carried, and used drugs all day from sun up to sun down never once getting "stopped and frisked."

Marijuana violations and punishments were treated similarly to that for cocaine use (cited with the schedule1 drug designation). And although marijuana has been legalized and decriminalized in many States across America, there has been no widespread retroactive reduction of sentencing or the wiping clean of the Records for those convicted (until most recently, with a "few" being pardoned by President Biden). Again, affecting and preventing mostly people of my heritage from being able to get certain particular "government" jobs and employment that can have a positive outcome on our financial situations and our overall general communities.

By contrast, the "Opioid epidemic," primarily affecting the "poor White" communities, is looked upon as a "disease" (not a crime) that requires treatment and that they should be "healed" and not stigmatized with criminal records that might affect their financial futures. I thought any and all addiction was considered an "illness." This is just another example of the "double standard." In this case, it's the "inequality of illness" for those of my heritage, with our again having to bear additional undue and unfair stress, which has been levied upon us from birth to burial.

So here we are again in 2022, going "Back to the Future," where you have State governments rewriting voting rights legislation and implementing restrictions on voting under the guise of another "Big Lie" (that there was massive voting fraud), with the lies having been disproven overwhelmingly by proof to the contrary. In fact, the over 60 court cases of "lies" initiated by former president Donald Skunk have all been refuted by judges (including many of those he personally appointed) on the grounds they haven't produced any evidential proof.

As a result, he has torn the country asunder and weakened this experiment in democracy. It's a personal choice by those choosing to adopt this lie out of their own selfishness to follow a selfish person. These people ignorantly want to have a Chinese or Russian-styled dictatorship right here in America. Just forget about our national symbols!

Congress hasn't passed (the John Lewis) voting rights legislation! But why should they have had to in the first place? Voting rights legislation was passed nearly 60 years ago by President Lyndon B. Johnson during the "Civil Rights Movement," led by Dr. King and others. So why at the time, was the legislation written so that the President has to re-sign it back into law every 25 years?

Before that, what happened to the 13th, 14th and 15th Amendments? They were specifically written to address the inequities and injustices imposed on the people of my heritage that resulted from their enslavement, and with them, the right to vote was formally and constitutionally guaranteed for all people! This is preposterous and ridiculous!

60 years plus into the future from that struggle for the right to vote in the 1960s (and roughly 100 years before that with the aforementioned Amendments), today you have State Legislatures once again attempting to limit it. We're "Back to the Future." Congress finally just passed an "Anti-Lynching" Law in honor of Emmet Till (who was brutally murdered nearly 70 years ago in 1955) when the people of my heritage have been lynched since 1619, with a notable upsurge starting in 1865. It's like being at war!

One of the worst issues mankind has faced throughout its history is the scourge of War. We visibly recognize its physical repercussions, from lost limbs to death. From the 19th century to the present, we've learned that stress takes its toll on our mental/emotional psyche and physical health. Terms like shell shock, battle fatigue, operational exhaustion, and post-traumatic stress disorder (PTSD) have been introduced into our vocabulary as we better understand how (daily) stress produces toxic chemicals that negatively affect our mind and body and, in some cases, our DNA.

Can you imagine having to fight a war every second of every day, from your birth to burial? Can you begin to envision the amount of stress and PTSD your body would endure during the course of a lifetime? Would you invite it upon yourself or on your family and friends? By extension, would you truly want that for any person or animal even? No peace, nowhere! Well, my friends, that's what has been imposed on the people who share my heritage! The amount of stress and PTSD we are forced to contend with is overwhelming! It's really not an exaggeration. It's a fact of our daily lives.

(The Hope Of "Star Trek")

One of my all-time favorite TV shows is the "Star Trek" series. It's been an encouraging symbol of what a future "Global Society" on our shared planet could, should, or would be like if we were to, for example, lived up to the American slogan and current farce of "E-Pluribus Unum." Most likely, I've viewed every episode from all 5 editions at least a couple times.

Recently, however, I noticed certain subliminal racial disparities even there. For example, there is a tendency to represent the darker species or inhabitants of the universe as being inherently more violent by their nature. In the initial series, when they introduced the "Klingons," they were unabashedly and irrationally a war-mongering species, inherently desirous of violence. The last of the series I happened to watch was "Deep Space 9." Watching that show is where I experienced the troubling thought that made me consider whether there was an explicit, purposeful intent or an implicit, ignorant, unintentional oversight of American history as it relates to what America calls "our gift to the world" in the Art form known as Jazz.

(STAR TREK'S DEEP SPACE NINE…
A Subliminal Message About Jazz Groups In The Future…?)

Perhaps it's because I'm a practicing musician that it dawned on me while recently watching an episode of "Deep Space Nine" when somebody or a group of "Star-fleet personnel" visited the "Halo-Deck" program. The most often visited program featured the Jazz combo of vocalist "Vic Fontaine circa 1962 in Las Vegas. I noticed none of the musicians performing in the combo were people of my heritage. None of the historical original creators and innovators of the Art form were represented! I thought to myself, "Oh no, not Star Trek, too!"

They couldn't be insinuating that the people of my heritage have no future in the music we basically created and gifted to the world! That's when it dawned on me about the dark species and races, particularly the Klingon stereotype introduced in the original series. So, I started watching the programs more intensely. It was recently, perhaps a year or so later, when I saw a ray of hope. While preparing my dinner, Star Trek, "The Next Generation," was on, and I heard Commander Riker, aka "Number 1," playing his Jazz trombone. I looked around over to the TV and indeed saw a drummer of my heritage present in his combo group.

However, the subliminal message of "white" being good, safe, or smart and "dark" being dangerous, dumb, or violent is conveyed in Media and in general society as well. For example, in the movie genre known as "Westerns," generally, the good guys wear white and light, and the bad guys wear black, with the exception being Zorro.

Look at the "Lone Ranger" and his white horse, aka "Silver." You see it portrayed in cartoons, especially if you view the older ones in black and white. Many of them have been banned and can only be viewed on YouTube because of their racial stereotypes. Here you have the darker people and animals often portrayed as violent, slow, and inept or simply as the watermelon-eating "coons." There was controversy over these depictions as late as the feature cartoon "The Lion King."

You may have noticed the subliminal messages with regard to color in for example, cake. "Angel" food cake is white whereas "Devils" food cake is a dark chocolate brown. Why has dark and the color black been so demonized? You have the word "blackmail." In the Arts, you have the so-called "dark arts" or the "black arts" and "black magic" as opposed to magic.

Throughout history, mankind has experienced plagues, then came "The Bubonic Plague," which was labeled "The Black Plague," aka "The Black Death." We have cats, then the infamous unlucky "black cat" or being the "black sheep of the family." There is money, then there's "dark money" and the "world wide web," aka the "www.internet," with its shadowy counterpart, the "dark net" or the "dark web." And we all remember humanity transitioning out of the "Dark Ages" into the "Renaissance Period."

Here's something controversial to ponder. According to the Holy Bible's written word, God has always or "eternally" existed. However, there was that point in time that God said, "Let there be light." One could argue that God existed in the absence of light. Would anyone say that God had a problem with his eternal existence before uttering those words? Disclaimer, I have no clue as to how God existed at any point in His eternity, and the Bible says that GOD is light.

This final point I want to make regarding the exaltation of White and light and the degradation of Black and dark is something I noticed over the span of my lifetime. Water is clear. When it freezes, it becomes a clear ice. When ice gets mixed the dirt or soot, it becomes dirty ice. When I was a child, and someone driving hit a patch of ice and skidded or were involved in an accident, they would say, "I hit a patch of ice." Somewhere along in my adulthood, I began to hear the news media refer to that same type of incident as someone hitting "Black Ice."

WARNING, THE NEXT CHAPTER MAY BE TO DIFFICULT FOR SOME TO READ OR DIGEST. SOME THINGS STATED HERE, OTHER THAN THE ACTUAL SCIENCE, INVOLVE STORIES THAT AREN'T BACKED UP WITH HISTORICAL DOCUMENTATION OR ACTUAL KNOWN FACTS.

Chapter: 6
RACIST PEOPLE HAVE A MENTAL PROBLEM AND HATE THEMSELVES...
...But they can be healed!

Humans, or mankind, are called "Homo Sapiens-Sapiens," which means "Thinking Man." When confronted with a given set of circumstances, we can through our brain's neural network system, process the information, then draw conclusions. An original conclusion could be subjected to further scrutiny, development or evolve and change from what we originally thought. We're not necessarily fixed in our point of view.

Look at the old argument stating the world is flat. New information revealed the planet as being round or globally shaped. However, as we look across the horizon, our eyes suggest the world is flat. Western civilization is generally ignorant to the information that our Alkebulan ancestors had crossed the Atlantic Ocean into what is now called North America (aka the huge Olmec heads found in Mexico). The "Flat Earth" theory was propagated during the time of the European exploration period, when sailors often failed to return, and those observing them sail away watched until they could no longer see evidence of the ship mast. They concluded the ship fell off the edge of the Earth.

In retrospect did their argument really hold water? Was "common sense" actually exercised with the "edge" theory? Didn't they actually observe a gradual sinking of the ship rather than an abrupt fall off? I suggest they didn't use the logic part of common sense. Earlier, I stated that common sense ain't common these days. Well, it seems it wasn't so common then, either. I find it interestingly ignorant that the "Flat Earth theory" had recently re-emerged. Have you heard, "The more things change, the more they stay the same?"

There are times when we Homo Sapiens-Sapiens literally "think" things through, especially before making a big decision. I'm sure you've heard people say, "Let me think about it first." I recall back in kindergarten or first grade, my teacher saying, "Let's put on our thinking caps." Perhaps I'm dating myself. Have you heard anyone utter, "I used to think that...?" All animals have instincts. However, humans have a greater ability to get new information and process it. The failure to do so may increase our chances of making a poor choice or decision and thereby experience an unfavorable result. Sometimes, after "thinking it over," we might even change our mind.

We've not only changed our minds but also our mannerisms or the way we act. We're not a totally predictable species. When we think deeply about an issue, we just might experience a moment of clarity. Usually, people don't think highly of you if you have a closed mind. One wouldn't expect any new ideas to come from a closed-minded person, and neither would you be a likely candidate for a "think tank." Generally, you limit yourself to various opportunities when you've closed off your mind. So, let's not be closed-minded here. The same can and has been known to happen to the racists when they open their minds and are willing to accept new conceptual information, aka Gov. George Wallace.

Throughout the historical record, "Man" has existed in several "human" categorical listings and name classifications that mixed and interbred with each other. Many humans today still share some level of DNA with our earlier ancestors. Do you recall the drawing of the hunched-over "dark" ape evolving into the erect "White" man? Darwin's theory of man evolving from apes (Australopithecus Hominid) is coming under scrutiny. In fact, I heard a theory that Apes evolved from the human line.

There is an extended line of the "Homo" or human genus beginning with Homo Habilis to Homo Erectus to Homo Sapiens-Sapiens man, with other species coexisting like Cro-Magnum man, Neanderthal man, and most recently, Austra Robustus, Homo Hobilis, and Denisovan man. Collectively, I personally call them all "caveman." However, they interbred and were all also called "human."

Humans of European ancestry currently contain about 4 to 6 percent DNA of Neanderthals and Denisovans. It's argued when you see animations of them, they appear lighter because they left Africa and stayed in the northern regions, thus gradually losing some of their melanin. However, according to current scientific data, current man, aka Homo Sapiens-Sapiens, all share a common DNA stemming from Homo Erectus via the Sub-Saharan region of the Akebulan (African) continent, with our common ancestor anthropologist named "Lucy" or "Degnesh" as the natives called her, whose bones were actually found in Ethiopia.

With that being the science, regardless of one's skin melanin content, we are still one people and one species. Therefore, I suggest if one hates the segments of our species with more melanin, it could be argued that they also hate themselves as well!

It is to be noted that the people of my heritage come in shades from light to almost white, cream, caramel to golden brown, to milk and dark chocolate. I leave you with a final technical issue. White, gray, and black are not considered colors because they don't register on the rainbow spectrum. So perhaps it would be wise to drop this color tag we place on each other.

(Races Are Like Roses)

As a common people and species, I would "speculate" that we are roughly 97% the same (this is my totally random and concocted number, just like being 3/5 a man). Before I falsely attempt to justify my percentages, allow me this supposition. If we removed all the skin from our bodies, we'd all look frighteningly the same, bloody and gory. For example, we've all seen pictures of the human circulatory and/or cardiovascular systems. Are you able to determine the ethnicity represented in these drawing? If you were blindfolded in a maternity ward, would you be able to determine the "race" of the baby by its cry? I would think not!

I believe the Creator chose to demonstrate variety among the species in creation, or in my opinion, things would otherwise be boring. Beginning with the stars in the heavens, each one is uniquely made. The same can be said with the clouds in the sky. No two are the same or the snowflakes that fall from them. It's not just one type of bird that soars above us. Some are birds of prey, and others are birds we prey upon for sustenance. There are a variety of animals and species of canines, cats, bears, and fish, as well as ants, bees, beetles, and bugs.

There are even a variety of soil types. Take the trees from the majestic Redwoods and the mighty Oak to the proud but tiny Japanese Bonsai tree. We enjoy Maple, Pine, pecan, and Walnut, Weeping Willow and fruit trees. We don't enjoy just one kind of berry. They range from Cherry to Cranberry, Strawberry & Blueberry to Boysenberry and Elderberry. We have great diversity among herbs and weeds, with some being a nuisance, like crabgrass and dandelions (which can be eaten), and others with healing properties, like ginseng and marijuana.

Fortunately, we have flowers like carnations, sunflowers, tulips, and the Venus flytrap. Then we have the beautiful and majestic "Rose," which is arguably one of the most recognized and respected of flowers. It's definitely one of the most popular and coveted. It's known for its beauty, distinctive fragrance, and variety of colors. I use this analogy for the "races" because most of us could recognize its fragrance even if blindfolded. I'm reminded of the saying, "A rose of a different color still smells the same." Whether it's white, yellow, pink, or hybrid to, the famous "Red" to the most rare and notoriously highly coveted "Black Rose."

Although I'm told the Rose's fragrance is distinguishable and has subtle differences, to the contrary, I believe if blindfolded to the vast majority of us, its fragrance would be indistinguishable. That's how I feel about the skin being removed from our body. The 3% I personally credited to the differences in our attributes are due to our levels of melanin, facial structures, and hair textures.

These are the decided and desired differences our Creator intended as with other species. What if everything was gray? On a positive note, at least we would have "Fifty Shades of Gray" available. I personally subscribe to a saying by the noted English poet William Cowper (1731-1800) that goes, "Variety is the Spice of Life." Well, the actual quote goes, "Variety's the very spice of life that gives it all its Flavour."

It is ABSOLUTELY GUARANTEED that some things stated in this section of the book will anger some people. Frankly, I'm understating the fact that it will be hated, despised, disputed or disregarded, dismissed and dismantled. Allow me to qualify what I'm about to write here by stating: Most of the following information CANNOT be backed up with scientific evidence or historical fact! However, it is a story I've heard that attempts to explain some of the reasons for the cruelty and brutality of behaviors demonstrated by the so-called "White man" in his treatment of the people, and in particular to those who share my heritage and other "minorities." As with most fables, there is usually a grain of Truth. With that being said…

(Let's Remember The Prolific Composer "PRINCE" And His Song: "CONTROVERSY")

Today, the people of the human species classified as "White or Caucasian" make up roughly 9% of the world's population and yet still control the majority of the world's wealth and resources. I've heard, through word of mouth and various media, of their "fear of the annihilation" of the white race as a species or ethnicity by mixing with other races or ethnicities. The following may not be liked or well accepted and most likely to be deemed disturbing, insulting, or controversial, to say the least.

I heard it said somewhere the primary reason the slaveholder was particularly harsh toward the enslaved men and still currently toward the men who share my heritage is because of his fear of mixing our race with his "White women." With the DNA characteristics of the enslaved (or of Alkebulan heritage) taking precedence and the offspring of the said Union demonstrating traits of the (formerly) enslaved. Obviously, the same would result from offspring born out of the non-consensual sex (the raping and forced prostitution) levied on our enslaved ancestral mothers (and fathers), resulting in a less than totally white ethnic offspring, at least cosmetically in most cases.

In some instances from those mixed ethnicities, the offspring was able to "pass" for White. However the latent "black characteristics" would or could show up eventually down the generational line if not carefully "bred out." As a result, again, the people who share my heritage come in an array of shades from light to almost White, cream and mocha, caramel, honey and golden brown, to milk and dark chocolate to cocoa. It's been surmised this is the predominant reason why "he," the White man, maintains an iron grip on his power today in America, and at the expense of "Black" men lives, so as not to become the "endangered ethnic species." The White species of humanity is the only group that must procreate within its own race to recreate "White" people.

(And The Next Bombshell Drops With: The Fable Of Man Verses Human)

The fact that melanin is what gives you "color," one angle of the story, associates the occurring condition of "Vitiligo" (a disease that causes the loss of skin pigmentation/color) in the people of my heritage. It's when pigment-producing cells die or stop functioning. Usually, it occurs in the form of blotches, but there are cases where the entire body is affected. It is also known as "Albinism." This is what is said to have initially produced the "White Race," aka Caucasians.

Another aspect to the story is that the word "human" is a composite word of "hue," meaning color, and "man," which is obvious. This implies that those without melanin, hue, or color lack the essential element of being "Human." Still possessing the title of man, just not human (hue-man). Obviously, this can be quite insulting! However, we recall that all the previously listed humanoid species were all called human. This story also accounts for how the "White man" became devoid of hue. I mention at this time that I learned that black, white and gray technically are not colors on the rainbow spectrum. On Star Trek, the Andorians species called the White man "Pink Skins."

According to the fable and perhaps a reversed version of "His Story," there were a group of humans on the "Mother" continent who practiced bloodletting. The practice is known to lighten the skin over time and was considered a highly aberrant and devious behavior that was culturally and socially frowned upon. It was insinuated that other questionable behaviors, including demonic practices and aberrant sexual lifestyle choices, were associated with it.

The general population sought to isolate these types of "despicable" behaviors from becoming commonplace and thought, rather than imposing the harsher punishments of imprisonment or death, chose to remove those practicing this as far away from the established community as possible. It would provide them the freedom and ability to create their own communities of choice while taking into consideration the already established community and society in general.

In what we now call the ancient days, the Akebulan continent extended significantly further east, including the areas known as Palatine, Israel, and Syria, and into the region known today as ancient Mesopotamia. According to the tales, these "deviant" people were sent well north of Alkebulan and around the Mediterranean Sea to the region known as the Caucasus Mountains. It was during this "ancient" period, after their deportation and resettlement, that the historical "Ice Age" commenced locking these people into that region for thousands of years. What is said to have occurred is they fostered, harbored, and retained a level of resentment and hatred towards the people of the Mother continent who banished them to the region.

During the summer season, we expose our bodies much more frequently to the sun's rays because we wear less clothing and our bodies naturally tan. It's especially noticeable in white people, but it's also observable in the people of my heritage as well. The opposite happens during the winter season when we cover our bodies over to stay warm and eventually lose that tan. So, according to the story, the people who were banished from the temperate conditions in Akebulan were forced to live in, adjust to, and survive in that cold, harsh environment and, over time, became angry, embittered, and cruel in their mannerisms and personality traits.

Over the span of those thousands of years, obviously, they weren't able to naturally tan, and their skin gradually lightened. It was suggested that their noses narrowed to prevent vast amounts of cold air from entering and cooling their bodies. Being unable to access fire with regularity, the meat of the game they hunted and captured often went uncooked and had to be eaten rare and/or bloody raw. In an effort to stay warm during the cold fridge nights, they often huddled and snuggled their bodies closely together to increase body heat. With sexual desire and the need to procreate being an inherently natural part of all animals, it is propagated that during this huddling, a man, perhaps inadvertently initially, inserted his penis into another man and copulated, thus giving credence to what has come to be called "Greek Sex."

But on the flip side, part of the reason they were originally banished to that area was because of their so-called "deviant" sexual behaviors. It's believed that this is where the "strong arm and survival of the fittest" caveman mentality was fostered and cultivated, and the "I'll take whatever I want if you can't stop me" was birthed.

It was this character type that was fermented in these people who came raging out of the Caucasus Mountains with reckless abandonment, stoked in hatred for self and others. Their thought process morphed into take and rape, steal and kill, to joyfully pillage and plunder, where weaponry was worshipped, and greed was good. Where it was also ingrained into their now subconscious minds and memories, their feelings of rejection and abandonment, then giving birth to their selfish and rebellious desires. Now willing to wreak havoc on one and all because of their feelings of resentment, jealousy and pettiness, especially to those they decided were responsible. Also, feeling that it's my way or no way and willing to bring it all down if it wasn't. They now lacked the all-important "human" quality of being humane.

It's thought being locked in those mountains for all that time is regarded as the main reason for their hearts being hardened, their brutally harsh mannerisms and inconsiderately cruel, nonchalant attitudes toward the people who share my heritage and for their conscience or subconscious justification for invading the Mother continent, by first hijacking, then claiming its knowledge and later returning to confiscate their lands, resources, and inhabitants along with their forced submission and dignity.

I'll mention a couple comparative generalities. From my experience, the people who share my heritage are far less tolerant of colder temperatures than white folk. During my 10-year tenure of working in a mailroom before teaching, at a certain point, I drove the mail truck in the downtown and Northside campuses. I observed white men and women sunbathing in Lincoln Park when temperatures were in the 50's and 60's. While in college, I waited tables for the best steakhouse in town for at least a year. When it came to ordering steaks, I noticed that white folk most often ordered their steaks rare, often insisting on bloody, whereas the people who share my heritage ordered the steaks done or well done, insisting no pink.

Over the last several years, in the discussion of the teaching US History truthfully and accurately, the number of times I've heard white folks say, "You can't blame me for what my great, great grand-parents did during slavery." Again, I repeat, I'm not holding you responsible, but you should be held accountable for continuing to suppress the truth of what historically took place in this country.

This is not about a guilt trip. It's about teaching truth and reality. What are some people afraid of? What happened to the freedom of speech? It seems many in the country would rather live under authoritarianism over the freedoms of democracy. I'm sure you've heard the saying, "What's good for the goose is good for the gander." I'm simply sick and tired of the obvious hypocrisies.

On the other hand, if anything like that happened in the story I just cited, then I have to flip the script and say to white folk, you can't blame us for what our ancestors did to you either! Fair is fair, right is right, and just is just. Right?

So, as the R&B song goes by Club Nouveau... "Why You Treat Me So Bad?" I restate that if we don't teach the actual truths of History, we're only teaching HIS STORY, and as the human species, we remain in this cultural rut.

(Today's Useless Excuses)

Should we NOT teach what's going on today in tomorrow's history books as well? Should we NOT teach about the 1/6/2021 insurrection, aka "The Big Lie?" Well, here's some additional things that should be included as more than just a footnote in the future historical books.

Again, I tapped into Google for a search inquiring on the number of "Black Men" killed by police since the year 2000, and of course, several articles popped up. I will highlight a few of them. In the first study from Chris Murray: for health metrics and evaluation at the University of Washington, in the medical journal "The Lancet," it cited information from US National Vital Statistics that more than 17,000 deaths by police have been misclassified since 1980, as of Oct 21, 2021.

They began recording their own numbers, which demonstrated higher death tolls than reported by the government, which stated that African-American people died at a rate 3.5 times the rate of whites as of Dec 9, 2021, and that deaths by police violence between 1980-2018 were misclassified by 55.5% and has been trending upwards since year 2000.

In an article by Deidre Mc Phillips on June 3, 2020, in the US News, it states, "Deaths from Police Harm Disproportionately Affect People of Color." In their independent study, they cited the governmental data was not comprehensive and found more than 1,000 people died as a result of the police in 2019.

The next article led with "How many people have been killed by Police since George Floyd," May 25, 2021, which states, "at least 1,068 people have been killed by police since the death of the unarmed man."

The following article by Mohammed Haddad of AL JAZEERA reported between Jan 2013 and May 2021, at least 9,179 people of color were killed, according to data compiled by "Mapping Police Violence," according to that research and advocacy group. That was an average of 3 killing per day. I stopped after reading the headlines of the next article by Laura Bult on June 30, 2020, which read, "A timeline of 1,944 Black people killed by police." These statistics are staggering! Most often, these people were killed by white police. How many times have we heard of these police getting convicted of their crimes? I first heard Paul Mooney say, "White people have the complexion for the protection."

This has been ongoing. Personally, I was only aware of one white police officer being convicted before George Floyd's murder. Since Floyd's case, there has recently been only one other white police conviction, as was the case of Kim Potter for murdering Daunte Wright just down the road from where George Floyd was murdered. This conviction happened only because there was video proof. Then there was Philandro Castile, an African-American man, whom dash cam video revealed was murdered in front of his wife and young son by police officer Jeronimo Yanez on July 16, 2018, in the Minneapolis, Minnesota metropolitan area.

Unrelated to the police, the three white men down in Georgia who chased down Ahmaud Arbery fatally shooting him while he jogged. This jury consisted of 11 white people and 1 black man, despite the black population being 26% of the community where the case was held. Juries are supposed to be reflective of their communities and the public raised questions over that fact.

However, this was an instance where Justice was blind and those jurors saw the facts for what they were and convicted the men! These men weren't older guys, either! Can you begin to imagine the fear these individuals and so many others were experiencing as they were being first harassed then murdered over such nonsense? Some people don't know fear because they don't have to live with it everyday of their lives. Others are simply in denial that these events are happening or just don't want to know.

Look at what happened over the weekend of May 15, 2022, in Buffalo, NY, which is eerily similar to the hate crime murders in the Emanuel African Methodist Episcopal Church, where a young white man killed 9 people sharing my heritage in Charleston, SC. This time, a young white man shot 13 innocent people minding their own business and killed ten of them in a TOPS grocery store in Buffalo, NY.

These are young white men of today! Where is this hatred being fostered? Some people say they're being radicalized on the "internet," in various chat rooms, and also by the latest media catchphrase "replacement theory." Are you trying to tell me that parenting has nothing to do with it and that communication within these families are so poor that they are unaware of what their children are doing or that they don't notice the changes in their attitudes and/or demeanor? I personally refuse to believe that! "Common Sense" tells me that parenting has a lot to do with this, either by DIRECT EFFECT or DIRECT NEGLECT. I can barely get this book closed out before another of these tragic events happens.

Most times, these days, you have video proof and still can't get a conviction for these murders being committed. For example, look at certain video evidence of what another young white male, Kyle Rittenhouse, got away with. This evidence was contrary to his claim of "self-defense" in Kenosha, Wisconsin. First of all, it wasn't his or his mother's business. Kyle's mother made a conscience choice to drive her 17-year-old boy across the Illinois State line into Kenosha, armed with an assault weapon, where he killed 2 white men and injured others because they were protesting the video evidence of a police officer shooting an unarmed black man in his back 7 times, thus paralyzing him. The "untried" officer seemingly attempted to kill the poor soul, evident by unloading his clip into him.

Video evidence clearly shows that the military-styled police in armored vehicles drove past, then up to this visibly illegally and lethally armed 17-year-old "white boy" and made comments to him, then gave him bottled water after the shootings had taken place. Can you honestly say the same courtesy would have been afforded a 17-year-old boy of my heritage? The "judge" in Kenosha then allowed Rittenhouse to select and stack his own jury with only one person of color on the panel. Rittenhouse was acquitted and set free. I thought jury selection was left to the attorneys! And shouldn't his mother be held accountable for something? No charges were levied against her either for enabling him. Let's compare this to another case of self-defense in the same city and around the same time.

The 17-year-old black girl and resident of Kenosha, Wisconsin, Chrystul Kizer, self-defense case against Randall Volar III, a 34-year-old white man, and known sex trafficker. Chrystul, then 16 and in need of money for food and school supplies, posted on the "Back Page" website after being referred to it by a girl she knew. Volar was the first to contact the underage girl after she posted on the site. She lived with him, and he sexually abused her regularly, sometimes filming his acts for over a year. He started trafficking her on the same website and took all the money she earned.

Volar was previously arrested in 2017 after a 15-year-old girl reported him to the police for giving her drugs and threatening to kill her. He was charged with child enticement and using a computer to facilitate a sex crime and second-degree sexual assault of a child. He was released the same day, not having to pay any bail. Court records revealed police had "video" evidential proof that Volar was abusing several underage black girls and that prosecutors received the evidence 12 days before he was killed on June 5, 2018, three months after his arrest and release.

"Common Sense" tells me that obviously, this 16-year-old girl was having major personal issues that stemmed from her home situation, made evident by the fact that she couldn't get food and school supplies and who's desperate option was to post on that low-life type website (that likely shut down shortly after that incident because of sexual impropriety); and after being "scooped up" by this convicted and now repeating sexual predator and offender, who also regularly sexually abused and prostituted her...

So let me understand this better! Is somebody out there telling me that this troubled little girl was supposed to continue to accept that treatment from this now-repeated sex offender? And this film indicates he was likely sharing and perhaps profiting on the fact that he was committing underage sexual abuse?

A Kenosha County judge ruled that young Miss Kizer could not use the self-defense plea after Volar had drugged and tried to rape her again. The

Appellant Court overruled and reversed that initial decision, and as of this writing, the Wisconsin Supreme Court is reviewing her case. Wisconsin, a State recognized for having these types of crimes and "Affirmative Defense" laws specifically for these types cases, recently voted them down in its State Legislature.

In light of the type of support Kyle Rittenhouse received, a group in Chicago has since raised Miss Kizer's $400,000 bail. To be noted, in Kenosha, the people of my heritage make up 42% of the prison population while making up only 6% of the State's population. Young Miss Kizer was in jail the entire time. As my oldest brother, the poet who didn't know it would say, "There's somethin' rotten in the cotton." As with so many other instances, there's something unfair, unjust, and unrighteous in these two cases in Kenosha. As I've also heard it said, "A blind man could see this."

CHAPTER: 7

THE ANGRY BLACK MAN: MYTH OR MANUFACTURED?

Many of us have heard the phrase "The Angry Black Man" propagated. Let me put this question to you. Would you be angry if you were, from the day your enchained and enslaved "ANCESTORS" set foot on the ships aimed for the shores of America, continuing through to the day you were born, and up to this very moment, your recollections and memories are that you have been constantly...

Abandoned, abrogated, abused, abducted, accused, agitated, agonized and aggravated, alienated, angered, annihilated, antagonized, and assaulted. Bamboozled, bartered, bashed, battered, battue, beaten up & beat down, beheaded, beleaguered, belittled, berated, blindsided, blood-bathed, boggled, broken, bruised, brutalized, burned and butchered. Carnaged, cheapened, cheated, coerced, co-intelled, collaborated against, condemned, consigned, contended, copied, criminalized, critiqued, criticized, crucified, cut down and cut to pieces. Damned, debased, debunked, dejected, deleted, demoted, deprived, desecrated, detained, devalued, devastated, disavowed, disemboweled, disenfranchised, disengaged, disfigured, dismembered, disparaged, disqualified, disregarded, disrespected, disseminated, doomed and drugged. Emasculated, enchained, enslaved, eradicated, executed, experimented on, exterminated, falsely accused, followed, forsaken, fucked with & fucked over, gangstered, genocide and gorged. Haggled over, hanged, harassed, hard-pressed, hassled, hated, hecatombed, hoodwinked, humiliated and hunted. Incarcerated, incriminated, indicted, infringed upon, ignored, interrogated, intimidated, insulted and irritated. Jacked up & jumped on, killed, kneed on the neck, labeled, lambasted, lied on, lied to, liquidated, and lynched. Manipulated, misguided, misled, misrepresented, mowed down, murdered and mass murdered, mutilated, neutered, nullified, obfuscated, ostracized, overlooked, overqualified, penalized, perjured, persecuted, picked apart & picked on, plundered, programmed, pogrom, poisoned, politicized, preyed upon, prodded, product, provoked, purged and put to death. Queried, questioned, radicalized, raped, redlined, redistricted, redistributed, ridiculed, ripped off and robbed. Screamed at, scrutinized, segregated, shot down, slain, slandered, slaughtered, sold, spat & spied on, stagnated, stalked, stifled, stigmatized, stolen, stopped and frisked, strangled, stressed and strained, subjugated and surveilled. Targeted, tarred & feathered, taunted, torn apart, tortured, toxic-stressed, and troubled. Undereducated, underemployed, underrated, undignified, unqualified, upset, victimized and vilified, whipped, wiped out, worried, xenophobialized, zeroed in on, and zoned out of...!

...I have to ask, Honestly...WOULD YOU BE ANGRY...?

Chapter: 8

DONALD SKUNK...

"PRINCE OF THE POWER OF THE AIR"

Ephesians 2:1-2

(The Devil Is A Liar And The Truth Is Not In Him: John 8:44)

Since the late 1800s, inventors like Marconi and Tesla's usage of electricity, the radio, and the airwaves, the world has been connected in such a way that has made it relatively smaller. It's become so much easier to contact almost anyone on the planet, regardless of their location. Today with the extraordinary advances in science and technologies, we now have the ability to instantly contact each other with lightweight devices at our disposal, with most fitting in the palm of our hands. We've learned to harness the power of the airwaves to convey our concepts and ideas around the world, whether fact or fiction, good or bad. We have a greater power to influence people we've never met, with some individuals influencing multiple millions of "followers."

Unfortunately, many followers cling to, hang on, and react to the words of those they've come to idealize or follow. I believe most people would say that with the use of this greater power comes greater responsibility and accountability. Today's social media platforms are said to have some form of "airwave police," whose "supposed" job is to monitor questionable language and interactions because of this ability to influence, help, or harm others. To me, their job performance has been questionable at best when it comes to identifying, uncovering, or exposing the mass murdering plots of "radicalized" individuals.

From the election season of 2015, especially beginning in January of 2016, clear through to the writing of this manuscript, only one person has dominated the broadcast news and social media's airwaves. It's none other than former president Donald J. Skunk. Worldwide, no other person was heard more, listened to, and scrutinized. It would be difficult for me to select anyone who dominated the airwaves more than he during his time in the White House, and although I wasn't alive during FDR's presidency, from what I know of his media masterfulness, he would still come in a distance second to Donald $hunk. President Roosevelt only had radio and the daily newspapers. The number of TV sets in America rose from 6,000 in 1946 to some 12 million by 1951. There was no "internet supported social media," and the News didn't instantaneously travel around the world in minutes and literally seconds as it does today.

I feel Donald Skunk demonstrates a desire to be "Royalty" and the "King of the United States." I don't believe he'll actually ever achieve that royalty status of being a king (or dictator), although in my opinion, he figuratively became a "Prince" John 8:44. We were bombarded (and still are) with his hateful rhetoric, "Mean Tweets" and constant lying and misdirection.

He became the "King of the airwaves" and the "Prince of the power of the air." In the Bible, there is a powerful entity identified as such. In the book of Ephesians 2:2, it states, "Satan is the Prince of the Power of the air." Former president Skunk is the only person and entity unto himself befitting that description. To be clear, I'm not calling him Satan himself. I'm simply of the opinion that he's definitely under his influence. No one before or since has had such a grip on the entirety of the world.

He's been documented as telling more than 31,000 lies while holding the office of President, and no one has lied to the public more than he. This breaks down to over 21 lies during the course of a 24-hour day. With that being the case, there are all kinds of connotations, implications, and references that could be made about him as a typecast between the two scriptures.

Again, part of the reason why I didn't start this book at the time in January of 2016, which again took about a year to complete, was because of the election/distraction of this "wannabe dictator," who had just taken up occupancy in the White House and who I nicknamed president "SKUNK." Honestly, I really wasn't into this guy. Somehow, I wasn't aware of the many references made to him by a number of "Rappers," perhaps because I wasn't into the genre that deeply initially and perhaps due to a personal preference of music having a more balanced approached of the melodic/lyrical with the harmonic & rhythmic elements of music and because although the style's lyric could be about social and political (or religious) topics, what seemed to get the most airplay were songs that the lyric often demonstrated a lack of respect towards women. I seem to be more attracted to the "hook."

But back to the Donald Skunk, I had never watched an episode of "The Apprentice" and had only seen him in the "Home Alone" movie. He began to register on my "racist radar" with his pronouncements regarding "The Bronx 5," where I later learned their false convictions were finally and rightfully overturned, but "He" openly vocally persisted in calling for the death penalty for those innocent young men of color. I thought this was appalling and insane in the brain! He demonstrated that he don't mind spilling innocent blood.

(Thee Don't Represent Me)

Donald Skunk continued etching himself into my consciousness with his statements regarding the birth certificate of then-President Obama (which I thought was ridiculous). And after I heard his bizarre ridicule of the handicapped reporter and his comment on "grabbing women by the pussy," I concluded he was mentally unfit to serve and wouldn't last past the first primary, let alone become "President" of our "great" nation. I felt it was only "common sense" that the American people would never permit such a crass, insensitive, and obvious racist hold the most important and highest office in the country and, arguably, the world.

How could Donald Skunk represent me when he was "given" the presidency after losing the popular vote by roughly 3 million votes? In my disappointment, it caused me to further question the "Electoral College" system, which I suggest should be dismantled because, unlike our voting in any other election, it makes our vote for President only "A SUGGESTED VOTE!"

Returning to an earlier point of so many people of today saying, "You can't hold me responsible for what my ancestor did during slavery or segregation," etc... electing Donald Skunk was not "yesteryear," folks, its "modern-day" baby. By the way, let us not forget how bad George "Dummy" Bush was for the country, but he seems like a saint compared to Donald Skunk; neither did he "appear" evil or as petty! Did anyone see the hilarious picture of Bush saying, "Do you miss me now?" that was posted during the $kunk Administration?

For those who feel I'm being partisan, let's review roughly the last 70 years, back to the beginnings of the Civil Rights Movement & legislation. It was solely about rectifying the continued injustices imposed upon the people of my heritage that weren't corrected by the 13th, 14th, and 15th Amendments after Emancipation, which included unfair voting restrictions and various other rights up to and through the "Reconstruction Era," the "Black Codes," sharecropping improprieties and the lack of education, Jim Crow, Segregation (Separate But Equal, but actually Un-Equal), the many Massacres, lynching and Drowned Towns, Redlining and housing discrimination, attack dogs etc... and up to that point in the 1950s and '60's.

Justifiably, "Civil Rights" are meant for all people, regardless of ones racial makeup, gender or sexual preference, etc... The painful point I'm making is the "Civil Rights Legislation" of the 1960s was "actually intended" to rectify those continuing ills committed against the people of my heritage since "Emancipation," which everybody else seemingly benefitted from "EXCEPT US!" The people who share my heritage have yet to see these "rights" fully realized.

In our daily lives, we, being the social animals we are, often get into conversations with others on a variety of subjects. Sometimes we agree, and sometimes we don't, and that's fine. We don't have to agree with each other on everything. It provides for a variety of ideas. I'm sure you've heard it said, "We can agree to disagree." However, there are also times when a conversation or debate is necessary to advance the betterment of the country. That's where democracy comes into play. No one ever gets everything they want every time on every issue, so, according to our Constitutional Republic and the principles of democracy, the majority of the people are supposed to make the final decision. In the way our government is currently set up, that doesn't actually happen.

I personally feel some changes in the Constitution should be made to make it more representative. For example, as I just stated with regard to the Electoral College, which, in my opinion, should be done away with because it totally contradicts the "one person, one vote concept." How else can you "win" an election by "losing" the popular (people's) vote by roughly 3 million, as was the case in the 2016 election with Donald Skunk winning the "Electoral College" over Hilary Clinton's winning the actual "popular" or people's vote?

Having only 2 Senators per state is not reflective or representative of the population either. It appears to me as a randomly selected number. I thought the Constitution was designed to be a flexible document and "amended" to adapt to the times. Is there anyone who could rightfully say that it's a perfectly written document? Some people, including Supreme Court Judges, clamor over the Constitution's "original intent." Who can actually say what original intent was when they contradicted themselves right from the start with, for example, "All men are created equal," but "men" from "Africa" were gauged as 3/5 a man? However, they were still called a man. Women weren't mentioned, so, technically, they had no rights. Wouldn't it have been more appropriate to have written, "All people are created equal?"

The science of the time did recognize we were all one Homo-Sapiens Sapiens human species around the world, whether female or male. We don't live in 1776. Currently, it's 2022! Could those men have possibly foreseen the advancements in science we experience today? Can we possibly know where our advancements will have us in 100 years? The writers of the Constitution, being some of the most enlightened men of their time, weren't perfect, and neither was their document.

Do you think they foresaw the telephone or the palm-sized ones that can fit in your pocket or radio and television? Did Benjamin Franklin foresee "horseless carriages," or gas, electric, and driverless vehicles or airplanes, helicopters, and rockets landing men on the moon and returning them back safely? Were the words abortion rights or assault rifles part of our lexicon? The original intent of the Constitution has to be flexible enough for the unforeseen.

(Donald Hitler, Adolf Trump…I Mean Skunk… I Mean Drumpf…
The Makings Of A Fascist Dictator)

Speaking of "modern times," I have a question for those looking back on the actions of their ancestors and acting as if they were the only white folk to commit harsh and hateful acts against the people of Akebulan ancestry in America. Here's another alarming fact! Can you explain to me why these "domestic" hate-filled, gun-toting paramilitary terrorist and other white supremacy groups rose nearly 800% in the country during and since former President Barack Obama's Administration? What's with that?

I often wondered how Hitler (the Austrian) was able to convince all those Germans folk to follow him and go so far as to surrender their lives in the battles of war. I now understand that it was because they were of the same mindset and wanted the same things. Basically, it was because they felt superior to other people and thought they were somehow getting the short end of the stick. Sounds familiar? Again, come so far yet gone nowhere! Have you heard the saying that goes, "You piss on my head and call it rain." Translated, it means you can't fool me with all your lies, excuses, propaganda, and your rhetoric "Bu//$#!+."

This piggybacks off this lack of desire to teach the entire American historical account. As a result, we're currently experiencing a type of revisionist History propagated by a self-induced mantra called "The Big Lie," where seditionists openly laid siege on our US Capitol in broad daylight before the eyes of our country and the entirety of the world, for the purpose of subverting a free and more than overwhelming proven "fair" election of, for and by the people, with an intent to end Democracy and this "American Experiment" as we know it. Then, install an unbalanced man as a "Dictator."

Can you feel the "Golden Showers" raining down when you hear individuals saying it was "Antifa" or "Black Lives Matter" or that, in fact, there was no riot and it never happened in the first place because the "demonstration" was an orderly processional through the Capitol as it would have been on any other day! "Rain, rain, go away!" And DON'T come back another day! Are you telling me that every day of the $kunk administration, there were daily violent protests and sieges on the Capitol with newly erected gallows and chants of "Hang Mike Pence?"

What's even more outrageous is there basically were no arrests at the time, and only one rioter/seditionist was killed. That's poppycock! Had that been the people who share my heritage or people of "Middle Eastern" or Muslim backgrounds, it would have been a totally different outcome, and I suggest it would have been a slaughter, with blood, not feces stained on the walls, halls, and stairwells of the Capitol building. The bloodshed would have trickled in the streets of Washington DC, with hundreds of bloody dead bodies strewn everywhere and a heavy military presence enacted and enforced through a presidential decree and calls for martial law. I declare that the headlining news stories would have read "A CAPITOL MASSACRE!"

I'm not saying that the single-citizen death to Ashli Babbett was a good thing. I don't condone any unnecessary violence or death. What I am saying is her death was totally avoidable, definitely unnecessary, and should never have happened! I'm only surprised there weren't significantly more civilian casualties. More importantly, Ashli Babbitt should've never been there in the first place! She and multiple thousands of others, including "white nationalists" like "The Proud Boys" and "The Oath Keepers," etc…had purposefully chosen to be in a position to hurt or be hurt. I could have said, "Kill or be killed."

Ignorance is unacceptable as their excuse in today's "information age." She chose to go along with the lie and the resulting program. Nobody forced her decision or choice because there was "NO LEGITIMATE REASON" for the seditionist riot to have occurred. These are simply the cold, hard facts!

Who encouraged these behaviors? "The Prince of the Power of the Air" himself fueled and fostered confusion, contempt, and criminal activities. I can't sugarcoat it. I heard it said somewhere "If you're going to tell a lie, tell a big lie!"

On the flip side, what if they had successfully overturned our government based on that lie? What would be the current state of the country? World safety would be jeopardized. Everything, everywhere, would be up for grabs. World chaos! No real beacon or light or Bastion of Hope. Is this what people really want? I'm a person, and I don't want that! Is this the ultimate goal of mankind and humanity? To desire that result, in my humble opinion, would mean there's a mental illness present. Those people would truly be "enfermo en La cabeza," Spanish for "sick in the head."

In that Capitol instance, I would say that the police lives or "Blue" lives did matter because they were in jeopardy of losing their own. We were collectively in jeopardy of losing our country and perhaps causing a general decline in our overall civilization. I recently heard on a "YouTube" TV media source that the United States is on a watch list "for loosing her democracy within 10 years". This shameful travesty was broadcasted to and witnessed by the entirety of the world, demonstrating America's actual status and lack of progress. It was American hypocrisy on full display, live in 4K.

And although the death of Ms. Babbett was tragic, I would say that it was warranted. Some people don't want to admit it, but the seditionists planned, plotted, then purposely pursued to pillage and plunder and cause domestic CIVIL STRIFE on that atrociously sad day. Here again, is an example of "changing the game in the game," where you "piss on my head and call it rain," aka "Golden Showers." This particular incident occurred specifically because of and for the purpose of a selfishly acting people attempting to maintain "their" own single-minded personal grip on the power structure of "our" country, where "They" and other like-minded people also pursued illegally gerrymandering State districts (an early example being North Carolina) while other States encouraged the falsification of State electoral slates. Some hypocritically legislated and enacted State laws to prevent free and fair elections and made it more difficult for (particular) people to exercise their fundamental Democratic right to vote!

Where is the urgency? You have the "House Congressional Committee" being stonewalled by Donald Skunk and his minions. And what is the FBI doing? Again, this is not the people of my heritage, but current primarily white "Anglo-Saxons" MAGA American Repunkicans of the GOP. These are some the same people from the Charlottesville, VA debacle.

It appears these Alt-Right organizations desire and are preparing for an all-out race war, with their paramilitary training and hordes of guns and assault weapons, and who have increased their membership nearly 800% since Barack Obama's Presidency. If you want to see any change in gun law legislation, let large numbers of "Black people" start buying guns and automatic assault rifles, then begin opening paramilitary training camps. You would then know what the FBI and CIA were up to.

There are legitimate Black Republicans just as there are White ones. But somehow, the Skunk Administration seems to draw its share of "MAGA crackpot type Repunkican 'token' people of color," with some seen occasionally at his rallies and, oddly enough, to spearhead his Alt-Right agenda like "Ali Alexander," born Ali Abdul-Razaq Akbar, the far-right activist, and organizer of the "Stop The Steal" campaign and Afro-Cuban Neo-fascist Enrique Tarrio, leader of the Proud Boys.

Then you have other media moguls like Candace Owens and Jesse Lee Peterson, who don't represent me or a majority of the people who share my heritage. You can also throw in Supreme Court "Injustice" Clarence Thomas for good measure. Of the video taped footage shown by the committee during the "Jan 6" hearings, and I watched them all, I didn't see any "pepper" spread amongst all the "Sea of salt." To be clear, I saw no "Black" participation (not even Enrique Tarrio), and although it's reasonable to think there had to be some present, I have yet to see any.

So, to recap what Donald Hitler Adolf Trump, I mean Skunk, I mean Drumpf aka "The Prince of the Power of the Air" has done, I have to return to" The Devil Is A Liar, And The Truth Is Not In Him" of John 8:44. To demonstrate, I'll present a listing of 40 pledged promises (lies) he publicly presented. Before I do so, here's an interesting tidbit of information.

First, it has become public/common knowledge of Donald's father Fred's discriminatory housing practices, but if you go back to his grandfather (John), you'll learn he was involved in the cover-up of Nikolas Tesla's free wireless "clean energy" experiments with at least 20 missing trunks of his known 80 that could have provided the country and eventually the world with free clean energy. This was in cahoots with the "Corporate" leadership of the then budding "climate killing criminals" of the Automotive, Gas, and Oil Industries. When you Google the "Trump" family name, they changed it from "Drumpf," the obviously German/Bavarian heritage to Trump. Why be ashamed of one's heritage? However, in my opinion, Trump does sound better than Drumpf.

Remember, the forcibly imported people of my heritage were forced to lose our original names! If you recall the television special series "Roots," it was there when much of America watched as the slaveholder had "Kunta Kinte" whipped nearly to death because he refused to call himself "Toby." It was in that series that the country also learned that was a common practice of the time. I've chosen a name for myself based off and around my given Anglo-Saxon one. Months later, I researched both names and found them both to be good and solid. I chose: Gerar Ammon Ma'at-Heru.

(PROVERBS 6:16-19)

"These six things The LORD hates, Yes, seven, are an abomination to Him: A proud look, a lying tongue, Hands that shed innocent blood, A heart that devises wicked plans, Feet that be swift in running to evil. A false witness who speaks lies and anyone who sows discord among brethren." NKJV

After reading that scripture, does anyone come to mind as it does for me? I'm only presenting 40 of Skunk's lying promises. Since he was voted out of office, we are still learning of new information of just how much of a scoundrel he continues to be. He said: 1. The Corona/COVID-19 virus would go away in the spring without a vaccine. A few hundred thousand people died after that on his watch. Rather than containment, he allowed for its spread throughout the county. 2. No time for golf. He played more than 250 times.

Reminder: there are 365 days in a year, meaning he spent nearly a quarter of his presidency on "his own" golf courses, which was more than any other president, costing American taxpayers more than $136 million (he also bilked the Secret Service agency for overpriced rooms).

3. Replace the ACA with something better. He tried to destroy it! 7 million people lost coverage, and he asked Congress and the Supreme Court several times to strike it down. 4. Cut our taxes with the super-rich paying more. The opposite occurred, he gave tax cuts to the wealthiest 1% and to corporations, which raised the national debt nearly 8 trillion dollars, which almost doubled any other President to precede him. The average citizen got a little more in their paycheck but paid more in taxes on the other end.

5. Corporations would use tax cuts to invest in American workers. Not! They reinvested in stock options and company shares with no increase to workers' wages. 6. Increase economic growth 4% each year. The economy stalled, and unemployment rose 14.7%, the highest since the Great Depression. 7. Would not cut Social Security, Medicare, or Medicaid. He proposed billions of dollars of cuts to the programs. 8. Said he would be the voice of the American worker. Instead, he stripped workers rights, overtime protections, and workplace safety rules; he turned a blind eye to employers who stole workers' wages. 9. American households would see an average of $4,000 pay raise through the tax cuts to the wealthy and corporations. There was no "trickle-down" effect.

By the way, is it just me who has a problem with the phrase "trickle-down," when it comes to the filtering down or sharing of company profits with workers, etc, as started by Daddy Bush in his "trickle-down economic" plans. In the context of a liquid, trickle down is defined as: flow in a small stream, as in a solitary tear trickled down her cheek. Or as: come, go, or appear slowly or gradually. Also defined as to issue or fall in drops or to move or go one by one or little by little. I'd prefer it to flow rather than dribble or trickle.

10. Promised the availability of COVID-19 tests Nationwide to all citizens. 11. He proclaimed that hydrochloroquine protected against COVID-19. It was rejected due to its lethal side effects. 12. Eliminate the Federal deficit.

He increased it by more than 60%. 13. Hire only the best people. He fired a record number in his Cabinet and other picks, the most in over 100 years. He labeled them as "wackos," dumb as rocks, and mentally unqualified. At least 6 were charged with crimes. 14. Bring down the price of prescription drugs. Prices soared across the board, with some companies developing drugs for the "virus" charging $3,000 a dose. 15. Revive the coal industry and bring back lost mining jobs. Loss of mining jobs continued as green energy jobs increased.

16. Help American workers during the pandemic. 80% of his tax benefits went to millionaires and billionaires; 21 million Americans lost unemployment benefits. 17. Drain the swamp. He brought in more billionaires, CEOs and "Wall Street" moguls than any President before him and filled various Department Agencies with people who previously lobbied against them. 18. Protect Americans with pre-existing conditions. He attempted to repeal "Obamacare," including those with pre-existing conditions. 19. Mexico would pay for the boarder wall. The estimated cost to the "American" taxpayer was $11 million dollars.

20. Promised to bring peace to the Middle East. Tensions increased regionally (especially with Iran), and his peace plan was (DOA), Dead On Arrival. 21. Lock Hillary Clinton up for using her private email server. He used his personal cell phone for official business, which could've been hacked, and family members used their private email accounts while serving official White House duties. 22. Promised to use his business experiences to whip the federal government into shape. Not! He caused the longest government shutdown when he couldn't get funding to "build the wall." His White House was in perpetual chaos.

23. Promised to end DACA. The Supreme Court ruled that his plan was unconstitutional, while DACA stood to deport 700,000 immigrants. 24. The promised 6 weeks maternity leave was never delivered. 25. Would end Kim Jong-Un's nuclear program. It was expanded. 26. Distance himself from his businesses while in office. He continued making money on his properties (golf courses, for example) and real estate, including buying the old Washington DC post office, which he turned into a hotel right down the street from the White House that hosted a variety of business moguls, dignitaries, and diplomats.

27. Force companies to keep jobs in America and enforce certain taxes if they left. Companies like GE, Carrier, Ford, and Harley-Davidson operated in other countries but still received massive tax breaks and put their money in offshore accounts. 28. End the "Opioid" crises. Americans are more likely to die from opioids than in a car accident. 29. Release his tax returns. He never did. 30. Tear up the "Iran Nuclear Deal" and replace it with something better. He never did. Iran enhanced their program, and he brought us to the brink of war.

31. Enact term limits for all members of Congress. He never attempted it. 32. China would pay for tariffs on imported goods. His "trade war" costed Americans 300,000 in lost jobs and taxpayers 22 billion in subsidies for framers. 33. Cut skyrocketing costs of college tuition. More defraud and profits for colleges resulted. 34. Protect American steel jobs. There were continued losses during his presidency. 35. GOP tax cuts would spur economic growth and pay for themselves. His cuts alone added 2 trillion to the deficit. 36. After pulling out the Paris Climate Accord, negotiate a better deal. There was no attempt.

37. Would sue women accusing him of sexual misconduct after election. No attempt was made. It's assumed he didn't want the truth to come out. 38. Promised to remove all the troops from Afghanistan and that we would always have a presence there, then left it to President Biden to hastily handle. 39. Pledged to put America first but deferred to Dictators and Authoritarians at America's expense. He ostracized our (NATO) allies. They laughed at him (us) behind our backs. 40. Be the voice of the common people. He made his friends richer adding power to the wealthy and harming American workers.

This information was gathered via podcast by former Labor Secretary Robert Reich, appearing on a YouTube video dated August 25, 2020.

(Biden Better?)

If we take a look at what's happened thus far under President Biden's Administration, he signed "Executive Orders" for protecting the "LGBTQ+"

community and the "Asian" community (due to displaced anger directed towards them over the release of the coronavirus) for the violence they've been subjected to.

There is nothing wrong with that. Let me point out, however, the Asian community has suffered beatings and attacks for about a year or so. A resolution (now law) in Congress and the Senate was passed nearly unanimously, whereas the people of my heritage have suffered for over 400 years of being terrorized, lynched, massacred, and unjustifiably murdered by mobs and police killings to this very day. President Biden has yet to pass an "Executive Order" for us, the very people who he had the gumption to have said during his campaign for the presidency of, "You're not Black if you don't vote for me." What has the Congress and Senate done except "NOT" pass any of the police reforms or voting rights protection legislation that John Lewis pushed for before his death?

Already, at least 4 notable deaths by police have happened on Biden's watch. Here's an annotated version of them: The 16-year-old girl who had a knife in her hand as the "Black/Hispanic" police officer Nasario harassed in her car; Anthony Thompson killed in a bathroom in Knoxville, Tennessee; The man killed in Elizabeth City, NC with mental issues, in the execution of a warrant; and Daunte Wright in Minneapolis murdered by a (White) female police officer for an unnecessary traffic stop (because he had an air freshener dangling from his rearview mirror). This trained "Professional" claimed she confused her lightweight color-coded "Taser" for her heavily weighted service revolver gun. By the way, those air fresheners were designed to hang from the rear-view mirror. So, in my opinion, the jury is still out on his presidency at this early point.

"Justice delayed is justice denied."

"The time is always right to do what is right."

"Darkness cannot drive out darkness; only light can do that."

"Hate cannot drive out hate; only love can do that."

Rev Dr. Martin Luther King Jr.

This applies for January 6, 2021 also…

Prologue

MALCOLM OR MARTIN

In one of my earlier subtitles, I emphatically state, "Come so far, yet gone nowhere." Despite our differences, one of the few things we all share that everybody loves is music! I have yet to meet someone who didn't. We may prefer one genre over another, but we all love it. It moves and motivates in an inexplicable way, from excitement to sorrow, and so often chronicles the historical record. And as a musician, I feel so blessed and privileged to be a participant in sharing the love of it to the masses. As I close this book out, one song sticks out in my mind that best encompasses my dilemma. The song was written and produced by the legendary vocalist Marvin Gaye entitled, "What's Goin' On," written between 1970-71, which, in my opinion, clearly demonstrates we've come so far yet gone nowhere.

So, the question now becomes what must be done and what are the best or most effective way(s) to actualizing these long-sought and much-needed updates and upgrades to our societal structure that will make America truly great in reality for the first time. There is no "Again" yet because, truthfully and honestly, the country has never reached that point in the first place. And for the people who share my heritage, for whom these natural human rights have yet to be effectively fully realized, how long will we accept this condition, and what approach should we take to make relief a reality? Should we go in on it like Malcolm X or MLK? Or would some hybrid of them be best?

Malcolm's approach would be more of my reinterpreted position of the "Golden Rule" that I've labeled the "Bronze Rule," meaning, I'm going to do unto you the way you do unto me so that you immediately understand what you're doing to me, which might be something you find that you don't quite like either or should we approach it like Martin?

You know, the "nice guy" turn the other cheek and allow you to punch me in the other jaw if you want because of the love of God in me that says I should not return evil with evil. But do I have to be happy with it and smile as my face begin to swell up, or the blood drains from my body? Should I, or anybody for that matter, be denied dignity? Can I demonstrate any level of "in-dignity" with your mistreatment of me when I show you nothing but love?" Or, since I'm trying to be righteous, can I show "righteous indignation?

I'm asking each individual reading this, which person are you, Malcolm or Martin, or are you somewhere in the Middle? What must be done to bring an end to this vicious cycle of disappointment with country and self? I'm looking for good solutions here, so I ask YOU, what would YOU do, and where or how would YOU draw the line? Remember what I wrote early as I came into a better understanding of the word "nice" and why nice guys finish last! Both decision and indecision will bear fruit. Will it be bitter or sweet?

AFTERWORDS

The intent of this reading was to first challenge Americans and secondly, all of humanity to take a good look at what we're doing to ourselves and dare to become better as the human species. To try and finally get it right as opposed to what history has revealed of our repeated Global failures. My hope is we would act like a worldwide Olympic relay team where we're working together for our civilization to win. I only hope this book will have the intended impact on people for the good while giving "folk" an opportunity to walk a mile in someone else's shoes.

I realize some reading this book might think, why didn't he write about this, or why did he mention that. For example, some sharing my heritage might raise issue with me calling America "our" country. I can understand their perspective because of how America has treated us over the centuries, some of which I account for in this book. My reply to that is, for better or for worse, this is where I was born.

I can't claim citizenship anywhere else (some say the exception is Haiti), and in some cases, if you're able to trace your ancestry back to "certain countries" on the Akebulan continent, you could be granted citizenship, and it would be great to trace my ancestral linage to its roots. Some people outside of my heritage might question why I didn't spend more time talking about the issues within our communities. It's because they've been discussed and written about by so many others. My purpose here is to share how, as a result of the many exterior issues, my perspective was born.

In the Forewords, I stated the issues raised in this reading would essentially be the tip of the iceberg of our historically confrontational journey in this land and encouraged you, the reader, to follow up more deeply at a time convenient for you personally. This was because I didn't want this to be a tedious and cumbersome reading experience. However, with each topic I raised, I could have written much more extensively.

My purpose was to introduce to the younger generations of and outside my heritage and to reiterate to the more seasoned generations these issues, wanting people to have empathy and giving "folk" an opportunity to walk a mile in someone else's (our) shoes, hoping that what you desire for yourself is what you desire for every living soul. Reality dictates that it's difficult to change oneself, let alone anybody else. With that said, I employ the "Serenity Prayer" daily, which reads: God grant me the Serenity to accept the things I cannot change, the Courage to change the things I can, and the Wisdom to know the difference.

To update a few things, since my initial completion of this manuscript in October of 2022, several self-publishing companies have offered contracts with all of them saying I have an audience for this book. Since then, I have reread and re-edited the book several times. I previously detailed a number of setbacks in completing this book later rather than sooner, causing me a bit of anguish at times, with the biggest setback being my entire manuscript was locked and irretrievably lost in my old phone.

I talked about my mother's sudden illness requiring her 24/7 home care, for which I was there serving her almost all day of every day until her death. The final setback was the unnecessary physical assault I suffered at the hands of my next-door neighbors. I was unable to add photos of the beating because the phone containing them totally seized up on me, locking and losing all the information I had in it. To my detriment, I wasn't into the "cloud" with its backup capacity at the time. Along with my hospital expenses associated with having a stroke and paying for my mother's funeral expenses, my financial resources have been depleted, which delayed the publishing process. In total, it has taken me roughly 2 years to complete what I felt could've been written in 2 months.

As I reflect on this journey, I've gone pretty much from being "helper to helpless," so to speak. Of course, an evolution this drastic is stressful. Regardless of those things I felt were setbacks, I realize how truly blessed I am and have been by the support of GOD via the people HE has provided during this most challenging period of my life. I realize how fortunate I am, which is an idea for a follow-up manuscript (God willing).

The final major setback in completing the book was and is the ongoing, seemingly never-ending shenanigans of former president Donald $kunk with the latest revelations involving his illegal taking and mishandling of "Top Secret and Confidential" governmental papers loosely secured at Mar-a-lago. I had to make the conscious decision to cut off my writings with this latest chapter. Only history will reveal if justice is served to this "wannabe dictator."

Finally, since I began writing the book in late October of 2021, many good things have happened in the country during President Biden's Administration, including appointing Ketanji Brown Jackson to the Supreme Court, passing his "Climate/Inflation Reduction Bill" and other legislation. He's being compared to President Franklin D. Roosevelt with his legislative victories. I see a clear hypocrisy being forced on President Biden that's not enforced on former and now-re-elected President Skunk regarding ageism and mental acuity.

It will be interesting, to say the least, at how our country resolve these self-inflicted injuries upon herself and what this Constitutional "Democratic" Republic will look like, not only after the 2022-24 elections or 5 or 10 years down the road, but in the next 100 years. Will America "finally" live up to her potential and actually be "Made Great," or will she dissolve and evolve into some sort of authoritarian autocracy or fascist state, an oligarchy, plutocracy, or some other hypocrisy?

Stay tuned! I just hope we actually begin to treat everyone in our country and all people around the world exactly how you (we) want others to treat you (us) as an individual living and breathing entity of a hopefully humane Human Race. And in the infamous words of Rodney King, "Can't We All Just Get Along." May God Bless each and every one of us inhabiting our "Living Plant Earth!" And may these writings draw you closer to Him.

Finally, Thank You, Don Owens, my high school class and bandmate and several times published author working in Hollywood, for your friendship, valuable knowledge and guidance, insights, and help as I wrote this. You truly exemplify the love God intended friends to have. And Thank You, Judy Dozier, another published author, for taking time out of your very busy schedule to read a couple of my chapters; for your insight in helping me to identify my target audience, for your comments to temper some possible offensive language and for helping me to clarify my point of view, and for your encouragement.

BIBLIOGRAPHY

1. Bernier, Francois (1625-1688). Article: 1st Comprehensive Classifications; French article in 1684, Nouville division de la terre por las differente especies ou race l'inhabitant (New division of Earth by the different species of races which inhabit it).

2. Blumenbach, Johann Freidrich (1752-1840). Divided the human species into five races in 1779, later found on crainia research (description of human skulls) and called them the Caucasian race (Europe, the Caucasus, Asia Minor, North Africa, West Asia); the Mongoloid race (East Asia, Central Asia, and South Asia); the Aethiopian race (Sub-Saharan Africa); the American race (North America and South America); the Malayan race (South East Asia).

3. Marcy, William L. (born Dec 12, 1786, Southbridge, Mass., U.S., died July 4, 1757, Ballston Spa, NY). U.S. politician, governor, and Cabinet member, remembered primarily for his remark: "To the victory belong the Spoils of the enemy."

4. Diodorus Siculus. *The Library of History*. Vol. 2, Book 3. Translated by C.H. Oldfather, Loeb Classical Library, Harvard University Press, 1935.

5. "HEW NEWS" Office of the Secretary, March 1973; Memorandum "USPHS Study of Untreated Syphilis (The Tuskegee Study; Authority to treat Participants upon Termination of the Study)," from Wilmot R. Hastings to the Secretary, March 5, 1973.

6. Vonderlehr, R.A., Clark, T., Wenger, O.C., & Heller, J.R. (1936). Untreated Syphilis in the Male Negro. Journal of Venereal Disease Information, 17, 260-265.

7. Skloot, Rebecca. *The Immortal Life of Henrietta Lacks*. Crown Publishing Group, 2010.

8. Team Ebony; Feb 17, 2013: Dr. Marc Barton; "Imhotep—The first Physician in past Medical History." Co-UK: Mikic Zelimir; Med Preg. 2008.

9. Toenquist, B. Sven (1964). IMHOTEP PYRAMID BUILDER-PHYSICIAN-GOD. Lakarfidn. PMID: 14229247. Swedish.

10. Browder, Anthony T. The Nile Valley Contributions to Civilization, Pg. 18.

11. "From the Lincoln Papers" at the Library of Congress (20, 206) Series 2. General Correspondence. 1858 to 1864 (840).

12. Thomas, Zoe. "The Hidden Links Between Slavery and Wall Street." BBC Business Reporter, New York, Aug 29, 2019.

13. Stein, Jess, ed. (1988). The Random House College Dictionary (Revised ed.), New York: Random House, Classic Housebook, Nov 25, 2008, pg. 28.

www.ingramcontent.com/pod-product-compliance
Lightning Source LLC
Chambersburg PA
CBHW060500030426
42337CB00015B/1658